Serendipity

Serendipity

Utilizing everyday **unexpected** events
to improve your life and career

Neil J. Farber, M.D.

Boyle
&
Dalton

Book Design and Production
Boyle & Dalton
www.BoyleandDalton.com

LCCN: 2020922389
Paperback ISBN: 978-1-63337-456-0
E-book ISBN: 978-1-63337-457-7

Printed in the United States of America
1 3 5 7 9 10 8 6 4 2

To Terry, John, Jacque, Stacey and the grandkids:
you have been and always will be
my inspiration.

CONTENTS

INTRODUCTION

Serendipity. It is often called by other names: Karma, chance, good luck, the hand of God. Some lucky soul comes across something that changes his or her life, and perhaps the lives of others. We all wish for that lucky occurrence. But often serendipity is only recognized as such after that occurrence is productively exploited. The term serendipity was first used by Horace Walpole in 1754 after reading a book about the Island of Serendip (now Sri Lanka) titled *The Three Princes of Serendip*, in which the title characters were frequently coming across unexpected discoveries. But how does serendipity differ from pure luck?

Luck usually happens *to* someone, whereas serendipity involves an unexpected event that requires *involvement*, or agency, on the part of that individual. Let me give you an example. Say that Rachel is a young woman who graduated college with a degree in urban planning, and after graduation she worked for two years at a construction firm building residential communities. However, the construction firm laid her off four months ago, and she only now has secured a job with the city that she starts next week. The city pays monthly, so Rachel won't have a paycheck for a month, and she doesn't have enough money to pay expenses. She is about to go to the bank to see if she can get a loan, but she has no collateral and therefore isn't hopeful.

This scenario ends in one of two ways. In the first version, Rachel gets the mail before going to the bank, and in it is a letter from her aunt Martha whom she hasn't seen in quite some time. Martha heard from Rachel's father, and she is impressed with the work Rachel will be doing. She notes that Rachel is probably at rock bottom financially, and therefore has enclosed something to tide her over. Inside is a check for $5,000, the answer to Rachel's problems.

In version two, as Rachel is going to the bank, she spies a bit of something under a leaf. She bends down, moves the leaf, and sees a penny. Rather than leaving it or pocketing it for change, she looks at it carefully and realizes that it has the configuration of older pennies, with two shafts of wheat on the reverse side of the coin from the Lincoln head. She remembers that a friend of hers collected coins and told her that some of those pennies could be worth a lot of money. Rachel takes it to a coin dealer, who looks at the penny, looks in his catalogs, and offers Rachel $5,000 for the coin. Rachel accepts and takes the check to the bank.

In the first scenario, Rachel had no involvement in the outcome, except to get the mail and open the letter. Most people would certainly consider this lucky. But in the second scenario, an unexpected event, the appearance of the penny, triggers in Rachel curiosity and the memory of what her friend had said, which allows the event to *become* fruitful for Rachel. This is what makes serendipity special: the individual is involved in creating something that is lucky from his or her actions in response to an unexpected event. Throughout this book, we will see how such unexpected events, and individuals' responses to them, created discoveries, ideas, and/or situations that benefited the person who was able to recognize the events.

Recorded cases of serendipity most often involve scientific discoveries, which is not surprising, given that scientists are specifically trained to be observant and how to scientifically investigate unexpected events. Louis Pasteur said, "In the field of observation, chance favors only the prepared mind." Yet, even scientists can sometimes lack the observational skills, intuition, and perhaps most importantly, the curiosity and ability to make connections, needed in order to delve into the mysteries of the unexpected occurrence. One example of this led to the invention of the microwave oven.

Percy L. Spencer was an engineer at Raytheon, Inc. in 1946, leading a division of 5,000 employees involved in the development of magnetron tubes for a radar microwave system. He was trying to build a radar set that was more sensitive than the current ones for the purpose of detecting planes and missiles at greater distances. He was an amazing individual, having left grammar school at age seven to help his family, and then educating himself with textbooks. With the help of the U.S. Navy, he became an engineer and one of the world's leading experts in microwave technology.

One day, Spencer was checking on the tubes' function and noticed that the chocolate candy bar that he had in his pocket had melted. Other employees had noticed the same phenomenon, but they had assumed it was due to the heat from the tubes and paid little attention to it. Spencer, however, was curious as to the possible explanation for the phenomenon, and he had an assistant go out and buy a bag of popcorn kernels. When Spencer placed the bag in front of the microwave tubes, the kernels vigorously popped. He made the connection that the microwave increased the motion of molecules, causing heat, which then popped the popcorn. He continued work on the device, which eventually became the microwave oven.

But it is clear that cases of serendipity go far beyond the occasional monumental (or sublime) well-documented scientific discovery. Discoveries involving archeology, geology, law, and even food abound in the written record. What originally prompted me to write this book was the recognition that my life was filled with such everyday serendipitous occurrences, many of them having a profound effect on both my career and my personal life. This work does not seek to give the reader a compendium of serendipitous discoveries (probably a more than monumental task), nor to try to characterize them, as other texts have done. Rather, I am attempting to meld my own life stories of serendipitous events with some examples from history in order to demonstrate that these events happen to all of us.

When I first became interested in this subject, I thought that perhaps serendipity occurred in my life to such a degree because of my training as an academic physician, which requires many of the same skills needed to recognize serendipitous events (more on cultivating those skills in your own life as we go along). However, as I talked with friends and family, I was amazed to find that every person I spoke with had a story of a serendipitous event that had impacted their life. It turns out that many people have these skills.

Introduction

In addition to the occasional case of the monumental unexpected occurrence that may be researched and exploited, situations may arise that also lead to a useful and/or profitable outcome. One can know what one wants to achieve but be unable to get to that outcome. At times, through careful thought and experimentation, or sometimes by chance, the way to proceed may appear. As I mentioned, my career has been that of an academic physician: seeing patients in a general internal medicine practice, performing research studies using surveys of physicians and patients to explore values and attitudes about communication and ethical conflicts, and teaching, all in a university hospital or affiliate community hospital.

In 1991, after having published several studies on physicians' attitudes about conflicts they had between their dual obligations to the individual patient and protecting society in general, I was thinking about the studies we had conducted on breaching confidentiality—that is, informing the police about a patient who had committed or intended to commit a violent crime. These were studies done using hypothetical scenarios with residents as the test subjects. One typical hypothetical scenario was a resident with a patient who admits during a visit that he had robbed a bank at gunpoint the previous month. The patient tells the resident that he did it because his sick mother needed money for her care, and that he would never do something like that again. Does the resident inform the police of the crime? Both ethics and the law say that a past crime should not be disclosed because of the patient-physician relationship and need for confidentiality.

In considering these studies, I began to contemplate the most extreme damage that could be done to a patient if the physician felt the need to comply with certain laws or obligations from society. The result of that line of thinking was my realization that these studies should be adjusted to explore physicians' attitudes about—and willingness to actually participate in—lethal injection for the purpose of capital punishment. In so doing, we found that the majority of physicians in the first survey approved of their colleagues' involvement in the various aspects of capital punishment. Almost one-third of the physicians who responded to the second survey, wherein we asked if physicians would participate in a lethal injection themselves, stated that they would be likely to participate in the process of capital punishment. Initially I was appalled to discover that physicians would condone and, for many, be willing to be involved in the death of a person.

After publication of this research, however, these findings were reported on by the media. This led to lobbying by many groups to change legislation so physicians could not be involved in their states' capital punishments.

Leading up to that outcome, I was able to generate an idea, adjust my processes to act on that idea, and discover important information—information that eventually enhanced my career (and led to needed changes in legislation). The scientist Royston M. Roberts has termed this process *pseudoserendipity*. It involves thinking about a problem or idea that you have until you reach the "aha" moment when the solution or how to make that idea a reality comes to you. This is within the realm of serendipity because although you are thinking of the problem or idea up front, the process of bringing about serendipity does involve chance in finding the right direction or answer.

Introduction

In other cases, one might chance upon a discovery out of need or due to an unforeseen situation. One example in the food world is how the hot dog found its bun.[1] There are two versions to the story, both arising out of need. In the first version, Charles Feltman had immigrated to the United States from Germany in 1856 at age fifteen. In 1867, he began operating a pushcart at Coney Island in New York. Customers wanted hot sandwiches, but the pushcart was too small to generate a full hot sandwich. Feltman had the idea to sell hot sausages, but he wondered how he could do this in such a way that the customers wouldn't burn their hands. Feltman happened to see a baker he knew, Ignatz Frischmann, and explained his dilemma. When Frischmann said the only things he could make were buns, Feltman was hit with the idea to use buns to wrap the sausages.

The other version of the story goes like this: Anton Ludwig Feuchtwanger, also born in Germany and who also immigrated to the United States, sold hot sausages in 1893 at the World Exposition in Chicago. Customers couldn't handle the hot sausages with their bare hands, so Feuchtwanger gave the customers white gloves so they could eat the hot meat without burning themselves. However, customers often took the white gloves. Feuchtwanger was frustrated. One day, upon seeing a local baker, he suddenly had the idea to use rolls instead.

Whichever story is correct, it was the need to provide a disposable covering, inexpensive and preferably edible, that led to the idea of having a bun for the hot dog. In both stories, the invention

---

1   Chetwynd, John. *How the Hot Dog Found Its Bun.* Guilfors, Connecticut: Lyons Press, 2012.

occurred due to need, but there was an element of serendipity in happening upon a baker and recognizing that something the baker could do would solve the problem. Any serendipitous situation requires an open mind, observational skills, and curiosity and/or intuition.

One other aspect of serendipity is what to do with the discovery once it occurs. Is it something you wish to take on personally, or should you involve someone else? An accidental discovery or thought can significantly impact your perspective, and even change a chunk of your life.

I had been counseled several times by co-workers to write a book based on the research into medical ethics I conducted during my career as an academic physician. I have written over sixty papers, but never took on the task of compiling them into a book. I didn't think it would generate interest in the general public, and, quite frankly, I was terrified of writing a 50,000 word manuscript (most scientific papers are around 2,000–3,000 words). Then one night I awoke after a dream I do not remember, and from that moment on, I knew the book I *had* to write. You are reading it now. But between the *aha* moment that night and the book you're reading was a great deal of searching the historical literature, thinking, effort, and writing. With any serendipitous event, in order for it to become something of significance, you must have the tools and effort to make it so. The third part of this book will discuss how to find the tools or help that you might need.

Sometimes serendipity will cause a discovery or change that is initially useful but becomes counterproductive later on. Early in my career I was offered an opportunity to be a program director of the internal medicine residency program at a large community hospital.

Introduction

It was the perfect opportunity for me. The chief of staff was an older physician who had trained in general internal medicine as I had. He wanted someone to lead the hospital in research, be a mentor and leader for the residents, and generally raise the academic bar at the institution, all of which were exactly the type of tasks I coveted. I gratefully accepted the position and really loved being there. He was a mentor to me, and I was very productive in my research endeavors and teaching.

Unfortunately, a few years after I arrived, the chief of staff retired and was replaced by a physician who had trained and worked in the same hospital where I was the residency director. He was disdainful of research and thought of the residency program as a means of getting paperwork done for the attending physicians. A resident's role in a hospital is to learn and train in order to become a physician experienced in a particular field. Residents may provide some of the daily medical care for patients, but they are always supervised by attending physicians.

The new chief of staff brought me into his office and made it clear that I was to no longer engage in research and was to limit teaching the residents.

I walked out of his office and into mine, where I called other physicians who had administrative positions in area hospitals. I felt that I could no longer run a residency program in which I could not adequately train the residents to be competent physicians. I also felt stymied from doing valuable research. One month later, I had a different administrative position at another hospital.

It is important to know when to give up on an idea, discovery, or life direction when it is no longer fruitful. Preparation is helpful in dealing with these changes. The third part of this book will help prepare you to be malleable as you find serendipity in your own life, including what to do when you are successful with a discovery or when you find that a serendipitous event becomes less useful.

I caution that I am not a linguist, sociologist, or psychologist, but rather an academic physician. I will use both my own academic and personal experiences with serendipity, as well as some of the recorded literature on this topic, in order to explore aspects of serendipity that you can control and use to your benefit. My goal is to give the reader a sense of how serendipitous discoveries occur. In doing so, I hope to instill an understanding of how the process of self-awareness, curiosity, and an inquisitive mind can be useful not only in our own lives, but also in the lives of those around us.

PART I

Ready:
Serendipity Is All Around Us

Some of you may read the title of this first part and think I am being a Pollyanna. But looking back on my career and my life, I can identify hundreds of moments that could be recognized as serendipitous. I believe that such occurrences are happening to all of us on a frequent basis, although they are not always recognized in the moment. Serendipity occurs in the lives of both famous and common individuals who take advantage of these moments. Most of the moments of serendipity I have experienced are not terribly significant in the world order of things, but they are meaningful to me. I've included many personal serendipity anecdotes as a demonstration of how impactful they can be to a career and a life. They can occur incidentally, through introduction by another person—often a mentor, friend, or loved one—or as an answer to an issue or thought that one has been pondering for quite some time. We will cover all of these in this part of the book.

CHAPTER 1
THE BIG BANG

When most people hear the word serendipity, they think of the incidental occurrence which, without much investment of time, effort, or money on their part, brings riches and fame to them. And sometimes that does happen. One example is the invention of the phonograph. Thomas Edison was experimenting in his laboratory with the telephone in the early part of 1877, hoping to improve its sound quality. A needle attached to the diaphragm of the receiver accidentally pricked his finger when the diaphragm vibrated. Edison had the idea that if the needle could prick his finger with the vibrations, it could also create recordings of vibrations, i.e., sound, in a soft material. From this insight came the phonograph.

In truth, Edison spent quite a bit of time and effort on perfecting his invention. It wasn't until February 1878 that he patented the phonograph, and over the next decade he continued to make improvements on it. My own experience is that at least some effort was involved in each of the serendipitous events that occurred in my life, and they all had a significant impact on my career and on my happiness.

Well then, what are we waiting for? Let's go out and find a serendipitous moment that will cure all of our problems! Unfortunately, it is not nearly that simple. Multiple factors make it unlikely that any one individual will come across one tremendous idea, invention, or innovation that will completely change his or her life. Let's look into why that is so.

One In a Million

Serendipity implies that there is a chance occurrence that leads to the end result. That chance occurrence is usually uncommon, and therefore unlikely to happen to any one individual. That is what happened to S. Donald Stookey, a scientist working for Corning. Stookey earned a Ph.D. in chemistry from MIT and then started working for Corning Glass Works in 1940, where he experimented with various types of glass and ceramics. In 1952 he was heating a plate of photosensitive glass in an oven, trying to heat the oven to 600 degrees Centigrade. Unfortunately (or actually, as it turned out, fortunately), he accidentally allowed the temperature of the oven to rise to 900 degrees Centigrade before realizing his mistake. As he tried to get the glass out of the oven, it fell to the laboratory floor. But instead of shattering, it bounced around on the floor and sounded and felt like steel. Stookey had accidentally invented CorningWare, which became one of the most lucrative products for the company and Stookey. If Stookey had kept a better eye on the experiment and the oven temperature, CorningWare would never have been invented.

Chapter 1: The Big Bang

A famous example of serendipity in medical science is Edward Jenner's discovery of the smallpox vaccine. Jenner was born in mid-eighteenth century England and apprenticed in surgery and anatomy. During his apprenticeship in the rural part of England, Jenner overheard a girl indicate that dairymaids did not get smallpox; they instead got cowpox, a similar illness to smallpox in cows, but one which afflicts humans only with pustules and consequent scars, but without the deadly risk that smallpox carries. Jenner didn't pay much heed to this, as it seemed too far-fetched of an idea at that time.

Many years later, after medical school at St. George's Hospital in London and a successful career as a physician and surgeon at the University of St. Andrews, Jenner was seeing many cases of smallpox, which often took the life of the patient. Jenner himself had been inoculated with smallpox as a boy, and luckily did not die from the resulting illness. While seeing these patients, Jenner made the connection between his own inoculation and the tale he had heard about the milkmaids' immunity. He took some material from a cowpox lesion on a local dairymaid's forearm and inoculated it into James Phipps, an eight-year-old boy who subsequently developed the cowpox lesions. Afterward, Phipps failed to develop smallpox when he was purposely exposed to the illness twice. Jenner had discovered a way to prevent smallpox, and so began the process of disease prevention via a safe vaccination. If he hadn't overheard the local dairymaid talking about cowpox, and if he hadn't made the connection with his own risky inoculation while seeing multiple cases of fatal smallpox, he would not have developed the life-saving practice of vaccination.

Serendipity

Sometimes a momentous serendipitous event will occur due to the subconscious. That was how Friedrich Kekulé determined the nature of benzene and how it reacts with other compounds. This may not be a biggie in the general population, but it was a major discovery in organic chemistry. Other organic compounds react in predictable ways based on a linear configuration. However, benzene did not behave in a similar fashion. One evening in 1865, Kekulé fell asleep while thinking about what type of structure benzene must have that allowed it to react with other compounds the way it did. He began to dream of carbon atoms linking up with one another and forming chains, as they usually do. However, in the dream, the carbon atom chains morphed into snakes, and one of the snakes chased its tail, grabbing it with its teeth. Kekulé awoke with a start with the answer to the problem: benzene forms a ring of carbon atoms, which is why its behavior is different from linear carbon atom formations. Kekulé had been working on the benzene problem for years without success until he happened to have this dream. We shall see later that some authors actually advocate allowing our subconscious free rein in discovery.

Occurrences of serendipity on a monumental scale are infrequent at best due to the inherent randomness of the inciting event or the necessity of a number of chance events lining up in order for the serendipity to be fully realized. But they do happen, and when they do, the results are spectacular. The most monumental serendipity that I have ever encountered personally was the result of a series of events that perfectly aligned to change my life forever.

In the summer of 1975, I was a fourth-year medical student at the University of Pennsylvania School of Medicine. I had been invited up to my roommate's parents' summer home on Bantam Lake, Connecticut, for the July Fourth weekend. It was a beautiful weekend; the weather was absolutely perfect. However, as is often the case in the Northeast, the great weather gave way to a rainstorm all along the East Coast that lasted for several days. On Sunday, July 6, I was getting ready to head back to Philadelphia to return to the nephrology rotation that I was on. It was raining very hard along the coast. My roommate explained that his parents would take me to the Grand Central railroad station so I could take the train into Grand Central Station in New York City. There, I would catch two subways on different lines to get to the Amtrak station on Sixth Avenue, which would take me back to Philadelphia.

All was going well after I got off the first subway at the station where I needed to catch the second subway to the Amtrak train station. But as I got to the platform, there was a subway train sitting in the station with its doors open but no lights on. Being the cautious type, I was not about to get on a New York City subway without adequate lighting. Suddenly, the doors closed, the subway pulled out, and the lights came on. Another subway train then pulled in, this one with its lights on. I got on this train, sat down, and waited for about ten minutes. There was an announcement indicating that there would be no further service on the line due to track flooding. I got my gear together, got out of the station, and walked the six blocks to the Amtrak station, only to get there five minutes too late for the train I was planning on taking. Exasperated, I got on the next train.

Unbeknownst to me, my future wife, Terry, was with her parents visiting a friend who lived in upstate New York. They, too, were late getting to the Amtrak station because of the weather and had to take the next train. As I was sitting in my seat, I heard a conversation about medical malpractice between two people in front of me. I was intent on ignoring what was being said, but the man said something blatantly incorrect and I couldn't help but want to chime in. I moved to the seat in front of me. There sat the most beautiful young woman I had ever met.

I introduced myself and I learned that the young woman's name was Terry. As I got involved in the conversation, it became clear that she was witty, bright, and very passionate about what she believed. I was awestruck, as I had never met anyone like her. As we neared Philadelphia, Terry asked if I knew of anything to do that week in Philadelphia. I told her I had two tickets to the Robin Hood Dell, an open-air shell where concerts were held, for that Tuesday night. The Philadelphia Orchestra played free concerts there all summer. She indicated that she had relatives visiting from out of town, and she needed to ask them if it was okay if she went with me. She gave me her phone number and asked that I call her on Monday night.

On Monday the weather continued to be poor with severe rainstorms all day. The Philadelphia Orchestra made an announcement that afternoon: the Van Cliburn concert (the highlight of the summer season) had been postponed until Tuesday, so the concert that had been scheduled for Tuesday (the one I had tickets to see) had been canceled. I was crushed as I worried that this would ruin my plans with Terry. I reached for the phone to call her. I planned to tell her that I'd really had tickets for Tuesday night before they were canceled, and to ask her if she'd like to do something else. But before I could call Terry, the phone rang. It was another girl whom I had dated for a while. Our relationship didn't work out, but we still remained good friends. She told me she had tickets for the (you guessed it!) Van Cliburn concert for Monday night, but now that it had been moved to Tuesday night she had a conflict and could not go. She asked if I could use two tickets to the Van Cliburn concert for Tuesday night. I accepted the tickets, called Terry, and we went to the Van Cliburn concert. We dated for about three more weeks before I knew she was the one. When I told her that we were going to end up married, she told me she already knew. We married the following May. When I saw her walking down the aisle I had never felt more joy and love. We have been married ever since.

Sometimes the lining up of fate rewards you twice over. Such has happened to me. I was fairly well known for my work in medical ethics, but I had never had rigorous training in the field. I came about it from the side, so to speak, which I will explain in the next chapter. But I did have friends who had been trained in and were well known in the medical field. One of them was Dan Sulmasy, who was trained in and practiced academic general internal medicine as I did, and who also conducted research in medical ethics. Dan was on the Ethics Committee of the American College of Physicians (ACP), the largest and most prestigious organization for both general internists and subspecialists. Dan was going off the committee (his term was up) and he was asked to nominate someone to take his place. I was a logical choice since he knew my work and I lived in the Philadelphia area. I was nominated and accepted the position.

The Ethics Committee of the ACP has several functions: it reviews the ethical issues of its members, develops papers on ethical issues, and conducts workshops on medical ethics at the annual meeting of the organization. After I had been on the committee for a couple of years, it was decided that we should develop a workshop for that year's annual meeting. I volunteered to develop and run the workshop. Sitting in the audience was a general internist who happened to be the chair of the Non-Prescription Drug Advisory Committee of the Food and Drug Administration (FDA). A few of the members of *that* committee were rotating off and they needed replacements. She was impressed with my presentation and asked if I would be willing to serve on the committee. I agreed, which led to a long and fruitful association with the FDA. If I hadn't decided to join the ACP committee when asked, or to run the workshop at that year's meeting, or if the chair of the FDA committee hadn't been present, these events would not have occurred in my career. So by keeping an open mind to the possibilities and agreeing to these opportunities, two serendipitous occurrences lined up and enhanced my career.

Such lining up of occurrences also happens in the scientific and corporate worlds. In the sciences, research and inventions are specifically built upon those who have gone before. For example, the Big Bang Theory: American astronomer Vesto Slipher demonstrated through observations in 1912 that spiral galaxies were receding from Earth. In order to consider this information, as well as other related astronomical observations, in 1927 Belgian physicist Georges Lemaitre proposed that the entire universe was expanding. Subsequent to this, in 1929 Edwin Hubble (yes, for whom the orbiting telescope was named) determined that *all* remote galaxies and star clusters are moving away from Earth from our perspective. Lemaitre therefore proposed in 1931 that

Chapter 1: The Big Bang

from the dawn of the universe, there has been a constant expansion, an idea we now call the Big Bang Theory. This theory has been supported by the discovery of cosmic background radiation, believed to be energy from the time of the Big Bang. Multiple astronomers and physicists were required to pull together multiple pieces of observational studies in order to come up with the Big Bang Theory. This may not be serendipitous per se, but the pieces needed to be developed and recognized in order for the theory to be developed.

We can also find examples in the corporate world. John Harrison was an official taste tester for Edy's Grand Ice Cream in 1982. He was one of the best testers they ever had, demonstrating an ability to tell the difference in butterfat content of 12 percent versus 11.5 percent.[1] He tested an average of sixty flavors of ice cream per day. One day he was taking a break from his lab. He planned a snack but had a limited amount of time before going back to work. He often had some ice cream and cookies as his snack, and since time was short that day, when he went to the company ice cream parlor, he broke up some of the chocolate cookies he had and mixed them with the scoop of vanilla ice cream he ordered. Harrison loved what he had created, but when he went to management at Edy's, they were less than enthused. Harrison decided to file the recipe away in case it would ever be needed.

The winter and spring of 1982-1983 were dreadful, with hailstorms decimating most of the peach harvest. Edy's wasn't

---

1   Chetwynd, John. *How the Hot Dog Found Its Bun.* Guilfors, Connecticut: Lyons Press, 2012.

going to have enough fruit for the "Perfectly Peach" flavor they were planning on introducing. Harrison went back to the file cabinet, retrieved the idea and recipe for "Cookies n' Cream" ice cream, and the rest, as they say, is history. Cookies n' Cream was the fifth highest selling ice cream in the world that year, and has been consistently among the leading flavors since then. It was serendipity on the part of Harrison, but also on the part of Mother Nature, that led to the creation of this ice cream favorite.

Serendipity can change your life and/or your career, and it can sometimes be associated with monetary riches or fame. But these extreme occurrences are also exceedingly uncommon, and there are multiple moving parts that must all come together in order for serendipity to happen on this scale.

Who Says You Will Be Famous?

If you are looking for worldwide fame from an occurrence of serendipity, you may need to look elsewhere. Although the occurrence itself can sometimes be world renowned, the person who first encounters it may not have his name on the tips of everyone's tongues. Although my studies concerning physicians' dual obligations to both the patient and society were initiated by me, others in the field of medical ethics have often been quoted for their involvement. (I did gain some notoriety for the work on capital punishment.)

Famous examples of this abound. Take, for instance, Henri Becquerel. Not a very commonly known individual. Becquerel was a French engineer and physicist who was studying phosphorescence and absorption of light in various crystals. At one point he was looking at the connection between the recently discovered phenomenon of x-rays and phosphorescence of uranium salts. Becquerel believed that sunlight or some other influence would cause uranium salts to fluoresce, or glow a peculiar blue light, which might somehow be related to x-rays. He wrapped a photographic plate in black paper, and then he put it in a sunlit area with some uranium salts on top. He wanted to see if the uranium salts were fluorescing, and therefore penetrating the black paper, when exposed to sunlight. The black paper would prevent the plate from being exposed to the sunlight. Becquerel then developed the plate, and as he supposed, the plate was fogged from the fluorescence of the uranium salts.

However, later in February 1896, the skies were very cloudy with little sunlight available. Becquerel decided to expose the plate anyway, and to his astonishment, he found that the plate had the image of the uranium salt even without sunlight being present. In a further experiment, he wrapped the photographic plate with the black paper, placed uranium salts on top, and placed all of it in a dark cupboard. Again, the uranium salts exposed the plate, and Becquerel clearly had an unexpected event when the uranium fogged the photographic plate despite the cloudy day.

He then was curious as to what was happening, and with further experimentation discovered that some materials are radioactive, giving off different penetrating rays. This is important, as it led to radioactive diagnosis and treatments of diseases like cancer, as well as its use in other fields. Other scientists went on to further explore the phenomenon, and Becquerel did end up sharing the Nobel Prize for his discovery. The person with whom he shared the Nobel Prize was Marie Curie. She, rather than Becquerel, is generally known as the person who discovered radioactivity. There are some scientific discoveries that occur due to thoughtful experimentation rather than by chance. But many such discoveries do occur because of an unexpected event that is then acted upon by the researcher (or another researcher who reaps the rewards).

At times, one may not have worked enough on the discovery that one has found, leading to unforeseen consequences. Nitrous oxide had been discovered in the 1840s and was being used primarily for amusement. At parties or demonstrations, volunteers would take a whiff of the gas and laugh and act foolishly. However, sometimes someone would become belligerent or even violent after inhaling the drug. This happened to Samuel Cooley at such a demonstration. He tried to fight with others, fell heavily, and was finally led back to his seat.

His companion, Horace Wells, noticed that Cooley was bleeding from a gash on his leg. Cooley was amazed, as he had not felt the laceration. This was the unexpected moment, and Wells took advantage of it. Wells was a dentist and realized the potential for nitrous oxide to be used as an anesthetic agent in dental procedures. He had a decaying molar and asked a fellow dentist to remove the tooth in front of a few witnesses while Wells inhaled nitrous oxide. As he suspected, the tooth was removed without any pain. Wells then arranged a more important demonstration of the use of the gas at the Massachusetts General Hospital in Boston. He gave the patient a whiff of nitrous oxide and began to remove a decayed tooth. Unfortunately, Wells hadn't given the nitrous oxide time to work, or may have given an inadequate dose, and the patient began screaming in pain. The spectators booed and Wells was forced to leave the demonstration in disgrace. He eventually gave up his dental practice, became addicted to chloroform, and committed suicide in 1848. He is unknown today. Although Wells didn't profit from or become known for recognizing the anesthetic uses of nitrous oxide, others did use the knowledge to help find a safe anesthetic for minor procedures like dental surgery.

Sometimes you can also be too far ahead of the curve for your discovery to be taken seriously. In 1846, many mothers and babies around the world died of a condition known as childbed fever. Dr. Ignaz Semmelweis, a Hungarian physician and scientist, along with other doctors in his hospital in Austria, were trying to determine the cause of the fever and prevent the subsequent deaths.

One day there was an accident in which a doctor cut his finger as he was dissecting a dead body. He soon became ill with a high fever and died a few days later of blood poisoning (widespread bacterial infection). Semmelweis noted that the symptoms and course of the doctor's disease were very similar to childbed fever. He noted further that midwives who attended patients in the healthier wards did not go into rooms where people had fevers, nor were they involved in dissections of dead bodies. The physicians who cared for patients ill with fevers or those who did dissections on patients who had died from the fever and then went to the delivery room had a very high rate of childbed fever cases.

The germ theory of infection had not yet been proposed, but Semmelweis concluded that the physicians carried some "particles" on their hands from those with the fever, or from those who were dissected after they died from the fever. He believed that the simple act of washing one's hands before a delivery would wash away the "particles" and could prevent the high rate of deaths from childbed fever. Semmelweis mandated that anyone about to enter the maternity ward had to wash and disinfect their hands first. The rate of childbed fever markedly dropped. Unfortunately, the other physicians did not believe Semmelweis's premise, and they ridiculed him. He was forced to leave Vienna in disgrace, simply because he was so far ahead of the curve. Today, the precautions Semmelweis recommended are an essential part of a physician seeing any patient in or out of the hospital.

What About Riches?

I can't cite any of my serendipitous moments that even come close to bringing in the big bucks, but some of them did add to my income over the years. And while big-time moments of serendipity are uncommon, when they do happen, someone reaps the benefits, i.e., profits. But is it always the individual who first came across the discovery who gets the payout? No.

Take, for instance, the invention of the vulcanization of rubber. Charles Goodyear was fascinated by the properties of rubber. He developed a new type of valve for a life preserver made out of natural rubber, but manufacturers rejected his discovery. The problem was with the natural rubber itself. In cold weather, natural rubber becomes very brittle and can shatter, and in hot weather it becomes a soft and sticky mess. One manufacturer told Goodyear that if he could devise a way to improve the natural rubber, he would pay a very large sum for the patent rights. Goodyear began experimenting with natural rubber, adding various chemicals and heating the mixture on his kitchen stove. He experimented for five years without success, selling most of his own possessions in order to continue his work.

However, in 1839, Goodyear was mixing a batch of natural rubber with sulfur and white lead. Some of it accidentally splashed over the pot and onto the stove. Goodyear expected it to melt, but instead it became charred after sizzling on the stove. Goodyear repeated this with a larger amount of the mixture and noticed that there was a rim of material that was flexible rubber; it maintained its consistency despite being subjected to heat or cold. Goodyear had stumbled on the right mixture for the vulcanization of rubber but was unsure of the heat necessary to produce the desired result.

After five more years of experimentation, he found that pressurized steam at about 270 degrees Fahrenheit applied for four to six hours was the correct method to get the desired result. He obtained a patent in 1844, and he eventually sold the secret to a manufacturer. However, it was the manufacturer who reaped the financial benefits. When Goodyear died he was $200,000 in debt. The Goodyear Tire Company was named after the discoverer of vulcanization, who never saw the financial rewards for this discovery.

Serendipity can result in rewards in many different ways. But it may require financial resources that an individual like Charles Goodyear can't provide on his or her own.

Some cases of serendipitous discovery require resources that an individual can't provide on his or her own. For example, laboratories and equipment available only from a large company. In 1931, Charles Getz was a chemistry major at the University of Illinois. In the Depression era, most students had to find work to help support their studies. Getz got a part-time job in the university's Dairy Bacteriology department, with the goal of finding better ways to sterilize milk. Getz believed that storing milk under high pressure would repel bacteria, and he began some experiments. The high-pressure gas did not prevent the bacteria from spoiling the milk, but it did cause the milk to be whipped. He then had the idea of somehow whipping cream in a vessel under gas pressure, which would eliminate the work of making whipped cream.

Getz discussed his discovery with a professor of chemistry named G. Frederick Smith. In addition to his professorial duties at the University of Illinois, Smith had established a small chemical company in 1928 called GFS Chemicals. Smith realized the practical applications of Getz's discovery, and the professor and his student went to work figuring out the type of gas and container to be used. The two launched the product "Instantwhip," which was an instant success. Instantwhip cans, produced by GFS Chemicals, were reusable. However, this was a burden for the consumer in having to return the cans for refilling. Eventually the Reddi-wip company took over the market with disposable cans. But Getz certainly profited from his discovery by getting assistance from Smith and his company.

Sometimes one of the workers at a company helps the company profit in a big way. The Flakall Company in Wisconsin in the 1930s manufactured feed for livestock using corn. The company was successful, but it would soon reach monumental success generated through an accidental discovery by one of its employees, Edward Wilson. The company had a machine that broke down the sharp-edged corn hulls by flaking grain into easily digestible pieces. However, the machine became very hot during the process, and employees would dump water-soaked corn kernels into the machine to cool it down. The water-soaked kernels exited the machine in a long ribbon of corn meal, which hardened and became puffy as it dried. Wilson took home a bag of the puffy corn meal pieces, and his wife fried them, adding salt and cheese. Flakall obtained a patent for the machine that created the corn puffs, which was eventually sold to other companies. In 1948, the Frito Company began selling Cheetos, and in the 1950s, Old London Foods began selling Cheese Doodles. There is an indication of their success in two estimates: Cheetos garners four *billion* dollars annually for Frito-Lay, and the yearly output of Cheese Doodles put end to end would span approximately seventy-two miles.[2] Yet Edward Wilson did not reap the benefits of his discovery.

So serendipitous events don't always lead to large monetary awards. But without recognizing and utilizing the unexpected events, one obviously can't reap any benefits at all.

Is It Worth It?

The answer is an unequivocal yes. Although big-time serendipitous events are uncommon, they do occur. If you happen to be in the right place at the right time, such an event can be life-changing. We will expound on how to recognize and take advantage of such events in Chapter 4. But for now, suffice it to say that with some effort, serendipitous events can really be meaningful. You may get both fame *and* riches if you happen across such an event.

Take, for example, Robert Chesebrough. Never heard of him? Most people haven't. Robert Chesebrough was a chemist in New York with a specialty in converting whale oil into kerosene. How-

2   Ibid.

ever, when petroleum was discovered in Titusville, Pennsylvania, Chesebrough could see that whale oil was soon to be replaced by petroleum products. Chesebrough spent all of his money on a chance to get wealthy by taking a trip to Titusville, where he could do research on the various products that could be produced from petroleum. Upon arriving, Chesebrough became interested in a thick sludge that came up with the oil when pumped. Several of the oilmen noted that it helped to heal cuts and scrapes obtained during the drilling process. Chesebrough thought he might have something. He experimented in refining the wax into a clear, odorless ointment, which he named Vaseline (okay, so now you know about his fame). He discovered that this was even more effective than the original sludge in healing cuts and scrapes.

As for riches, Chesebrough went around to audiences in New York. He would cause injury to himself and then use Vaseline to heal the wound, all while showing past wounds that had healed using the product. The use of Vaseline caught on, and Chesebrough opened his first factory to manufacture it. Vaseline is still a product sold every day around the world, and Chesebrough became one of the wealthiest men of his time. When Chesebrough-Ponds was sold in 1987, Vaseline was generating $75 million in profits annually.

However, you cannot take advantage of such an event if it is ignored. Remember the previous example of Percy L. Spencer who came across the phenomenon that led him to invent the microwave oven? Several of his colleagues had also experienced the melting of chocolate bars in their pockets when working around the microwave tubes. Yet they considered it just a nuisance, whereas Spencer let it spark curiosity that ultimately led to discovery.

Chapter 1: The Big Bang

A similar failure to recognize the significance of a find can be found in ancient history. The city of Pompeii was buried in over nineteen feet of volcanic ash and material when Mount Vesuvius erupted in August 79 AD. The city lay buried for centuries, as no excavation was ever attempted. However, in the late 1590s, Rome decided to build a canal through the region in order to divert some of the flow of the Sarno River toward Naples, as more water was needed. Domenico Fontana was the architect, and as his laborers were digging a channel, they came across some of the ruins of Pompeii. Fontana and the laborers failed to recognize the significance of the find, and the city remained undiscovered until more than 100 years later.

In 1709, a well was being excavated in the woods at Frati Alcantarini, and the whole shell of one of Herculaneum's theaters appeared. This was the city next to Pompeii that was also buried in the eruption of Mount Vesuvius. More excavation of the area occurred, and in 1738, King Charles of Bourbon sponsored a more formal excavation of Pompeii, which has continued up until the present. A historically ancient city was almost overlooked until its significance was recognized. The consequences of ignoring a potentially important discovery, occurrence, or idea can be significant.

However, when one does pay attention to such events, the rewards can be great, as we have seen. Gerry Thomas chose to recognize a serendipitous moment, leading to an invention that would change American culture in the early 1950s. Thomas was a Canadian who moved to the United States to become a salesman, and he became a marketing and sales executive for C. A. Swanson & Sons, which sold meats and other food products to restaurants and other companies. In 1951, the autumn and early winter were quite warm, according to Thomas, leading to fewer sales of turkey meat. Swanson was left with an excess of 520,000 pounds of the stuff, with no clue as to what to do with it.

Thomas was on a Pan Am flight back to Omaha and the company's headquarters, and noticed that in-flight meals (yes, they did serve meals to *all* passengers back then) were served in a metal tray. When he returned to Omaha, he was downtown and saw a crowd of people watching a television in a shop window. Thomas had a flash of insight. He connected the metal serving trays on his flight with the TVs in the window. He came up with the idea of a frozen meal in an aluminum tray, which could be easily heated and eaten in front of the TV. Thus, the TV dinner was born. If Thomas had ignored his instincts, Swanson would have been left with lots of turkey that would have spoiled, and America would never have experienced TV dinners.

Despite the disclaimers I have given about the rarity of a monumental serendipitous event, as well as the possibility of failing to reap the benefits of fame and/or fortune, it is worthwhile keeping one's senses focused in order to determine that such an event has presented itself. But even more important, on an individual basis, are smaller-scale serendipitous events. These are significantly more frequent and likely to happen to most people. Although they may seem inconsequential, small instances of serendipity can help you in your everyday life, and they may also be the start of something big. You won't know where a possibility might land you until you start exploring it. I will show you many examples of minor, everyday unexpected events that ended up changing someone's life for the better. I call this everyday serendipity.

CHAPTER 2
EVERYDAY SERENDIPITY

Unexpected events that can lead to a successful, serendipitous one occur to all of us on a regular basis. Though fame and fortune may not always be yours when they do occur, they still may be of benefit to you and/or others in multiple ways. I can't say that I have ever really become famous, and I certainly have not profited financially from all of the serendipitous events in my life. But it has still been a blast experiencing these events, and they have helped my career and my personal life in many ways, as you will see. Occasionally, fame and fortune actually do occur to some individuals. Okay, so I am still waiting for mine.

Take the case of the humble sewing machine. Many inventors had worked on variations of a sewing machine since the 1700s, but ultimately, none were very useful or successful. Then along came Elias Howe, who got the idea to work on a more useful sewing machine when he overheard a conversation between the owner and a client at the shop of a mechanic, Art Davis, where he was working. Howe had apprenticed in a textile factory in Lowell, Massachusetts, beginning in 1835. During the Panic of 1837 the factory closed, and Howe then went to Art Davis's shop in Cambridge. Howe set to work on improving the sewing machine, but was unsuccessful for eight years, and was nearly penniless.

After all those years of trial and error, Howe had a dream one night in which he was facing execution unless he could come up with a way to produce a successful sewing machine. In the dream he was on the way to the execution when he saw guards carrying swords with slits at the tops of their blade. He awoke and completed the idea for the machine. The machine had a needle with thread running through an eye in the needle, a shuttle which held the thread and passed it through the needle, and an automatic feeding system allowing two threads to be pulled through the fabric, locking them in place. Howe developed a factory to produce the machines, and he was so successful that he became one of the wealthiest men in the United States at that time, amassing over $13 million (equivalent to over $1.7 billion today).[1] So Howe had two unexpected events: the conversation that set him on the road to seeking the invention and, more importantly, the dream that gave him the answer.

Not everyone can encounter the one-in-a-million unexpected event that does lead one to tremendous fame and fortune.

---

1   Verstraete, Larry. *Accidental Discoveries.* Victoria, Canada: Friesen Press, 2016.

Let's take a look at some of the important ways in which serendipity may impact you and how they may occur.

Serendipity and Your Career

Even if not hugely profitable or leading to great fame, serendipity can often enhance one's career. In fact, in one study of
older adults using a brief questionnaire, 63% of men and 57% of
women indicated that their careers were affected by serendipitous events. [2]Serendipitous events have played a major role in my
career; serendipity actually was the impetus behind my decision
to join academia.

Early in my life I knew that I wanted to go into medicine.
I was always interested in science, especially biology. When I was
in first grade, I am told that I would converse with my oldest
brother, then a biology major in college, about the function of
different organs in the body (just as some kids know all of the
dinosaurs; in my case it was human biology). Both my father and
my older brother had that influence on me. My father grew up in
the Catskills in New York, the oldest child of a family that initially
engaged in farming, and in later years owned and ran a bungalow
colony in the heyday of the Borscht Belt. This was the area in the
Catskills where many hotels and small groups of cottages or bun-
galows allowed people from New York City to vacation during the
hot summers.

---

2   Betsworth, Deborah G and J. C. Hansen. "The Categorization of
Serendipitous Career Development Events." *Journal of Career Assessment.*
1996, vol. 4: 91-98.

My Father was brilliant and very interested in biology, since he desperately wanted to become a physician. Even though at that time our small town had only a one-room schoolhouse, he was offered a full scholarship to Peter Stuyvesant High School in New York City (even now the premier high school in New York). He started there and was doing very well, but had to go back home to help out my grandfather with both the small farm and the bungalow colony. The school told him that he needed to stay in the city, but since he was doing very well he was given an exception. When he had to return home a second time, however, my father was dismissed from the school. Since he could not fulfill his dream, he always wanted his sons to fulfill theirs. My oldest brother was also a role model for me, as he graduated college and enrolled in the State University of New York Downstate Medical College in Brooklyn.

Most of my spare time from elementary school through senior high school was spent exploring the scientific world around us with my best friend, Ben Malkiel, who like me was interested in science, especially biology. He had a stream in back of his house where we collected samples of algae and one-celled animals to evaluate under a microscope his parents bought him. I was always interested in how I could help others, and really liked the things that were happening in medicine at that time: surgical advances, such as transplantation medicine, and advances in pharmaceuticals for chronic disease. So I eventually decided to enter the field of medicine.

However, as I came from a small town in upstate New York, I envisioned myself as a practitioner (family doctor, for example) in that town or some other in a more rural area. But events changed my future in my senior year of high school. Our small-town high school (we no longer had a one-room schoolhouse as was the case in my father's youth) was able to capitalize on the small yet fairly wealthy nature of the school district. Innovative programs had been developed, and perhaps for me, the most innovative was something called Red Letter Day. At the end of our senior year, we submitted a list of our top three favorite teachers and were matched with one of them. On Red Letter Day, we developed lesson plans, taught the classes, sat in the teacher's lounge at lunch; we were, for all intents and purposes, that teacher for the day. I was hooked—from that day on, I knew that I had to teach.

I began to read about the different career options after becoming a physician and learned that academic medicine— teaching, research, *and* seeing patients—was a possibility. This seemed the most attractive path for me. The Red Letter Day event at my high school helped to refine my career path, and, in fact, it influenced the rest of my professional life.

Another example of serendipity affecting my career occurred during my second position as an Assistant Professor of Medicine at Hahnemann University (now Drexel University School of Medicine) in Philadelphia. I was in the division of General Internal Medicine, and our division chief held a weekly conference relating to various aspects of general internal medicine. All academic physicians develop an interest in some kind of research since it is required for promotion (advancing up the ladder from instructor to assistant professor then associate professor and finally professor).

My major interest started in the area of communication between patients and physicians; I still do have involvement in teaching that subject and have done studies in that area. One of the weekly conferences each month was devoted to medical ethics, in which I did not really have an interest. However, one of the ethics conferences was a discussion about how to decide who gets scarce medical resources when there is not enough to go around. This is a common topic in medical ethics. The discussion began to shift to the hypothetical issue of how to decide who should receive cardiopulmonary resuscitation (a "code," where the team rushes in and provides artificial respiration, chest compressions, and shocks to attempt to restart the heart) in the event that two people would code at the same time and there was only one code team. After a while, one of the residents in attendance spoke up and said that the discussion was moot, since they *always* made that decision based on the needs of the patients.

It immediately struck me that all of us have biases that come into play in medical decision-making, and that the resident was not recognizing that he possessed such biases. The feeling that I had at that moment was awesome. It was like being in a darkened room where all I could see was shades of gray, and suddenly someone turned on the light. It was almost blinding at first, but after a few seconds I could see everything in the room, as well as all of the colors. Not only had I not previously realized the fact that every physician has biases that may influencer the care of the patient, but I realized that this particular area of biases in physicians had not been previously explored. I was braking ground into an entirely new aspect of medical ethics. I knew then that I *needed* to explore this aspect of medicine.

I put together a survey that used hypothetical scenarios in order to explore biases that the residents in internal medicine held regarding decisions of who would likely receive cardiopulmonary resuscitation. The survey demonstrated that the residents held significant biases. For example, they were more likely to provide resuscitative efforts for a patient who was more respected in society. They favored a CEO over a homeless intravenous drug addict, even if both had the exact same medical condition. The results were presented in the plenary session of the Society of Medical Decision Making the following year, and they were eventually published in the *Archives of Internal Medicine*.

This led to a separate track of research for me that would eventually lead to more than thirty published scientific papers and a large amount of time devoted to teaching in the area of physicians' values. It was the unexpected event of the resident saying that the discussion was moot that led me to this field. I remembered my own residency, where many of my colleagues used unflattering terms for patients who had social problems like homelessness or addictions. In that instant, I knew that the resident who said that the conversation was moot was biased, and I recognized that many residents become tired, angry, and dehumanized during their training. I felt I needed to expose this aspect of medicine to colleagues as well as to the public eye. I knew I had hit upon something. It is terrific when you suddenly realize that you have a passion in your life, as I did for this area of work.

It is clear that serendipitous events can positively affect one's career. Many individuals have commented on these occurrences, even when the career is planned from the beginning. Col. Chris Hadfield, in his book, *An Astronaut's Guide to Life on Earth*, talks about the many different serendipitous events that had to occur to lead him to becoming an astronaut, though he had planned on doing so since age ten. Clearly, serendipity can positively affect your career. The trick is to develop the ability to recognize such events when they occur, and then learn how to take advantage of them. We shall explore how to do that in Part II.

Unexpected Events in Manufacturing

Everyday serendipity can also benefit an individual in other ways. Sometimes it may even be profitable. Clarence A. Crane owned a chocolate candy manufacturing company. Though normally profitable, business was slow during the summer months, as many people did not want to have the chocolate melt from the heat. He developed a sugar-based, non-chocolate hard candy, and hired someone to mass-produce a candy that was round but fairly flat. The machine malfunctioned, producing a candy with a hole in the middle. Crane liked the look of the candy and sold it with the name Life Savers. It became an instant hit because of the name, shape, and convenience of carting it around. Crane went on to mass-produce the candy and then sold its rights, with the candy eventually being produced by Mars, Inc.

Another very popular candy began production in 1926 due to a machine malfunction. E. Hoffman and Company tried to manufacture a round, chocolate-covered caramel candy that contained a large amount of milk. The machine, though, produced lopsided balls that the company felt were duds in terms of shape, but which had a terrific taste. The public went wild over them, and so Milk Duds became a hit. In both cases, the accidental everyday malfunctions of a machine allowed for a profitable occurrence.

Keeping your Eyes Open: Examples With Food

It is my firm belief that everyday types of serendipity are all around us. The problem is that many people overlook the opportunities that are presented to them, just like the employees at Raytheon did while their boss, Percy Spencer, ended up inventing the microwave oven, as we discussed in Chapter 1. Okay, so he was an engineer at a company and had the knowledge and resources necessary to make something out of his discovery. But one need not be an engineer in order to find simple solutions or opportunities in everyday life.

It seems that a lot of everyday serendipity (at least those written about) deals with various foods that were developed accidentally. Take, for instance, the famous story about Toll House chocolate chip cookies. The story goes that Ruth Graves Wakefield and her husband bought a house in 1930 in Whitman, Massachusetts, that had been used as a tollhouse and rest stop on the road between New Bedford and Boston during the 1700s. Ruth was educated at the Framingham State Normal School Department of Household Arts, graduating in 1924. The couple turned the house into an inn that they named the Toll House. Wakefield had written several cookbooks and was doing all of the cooking for the inn and restaurant. She was baking butter cookies one day when she realized she was missing some ingredient (perhaps cocoa powder). Instead of going to the store, she broke up a couple of Nestle bars, thinking they would melt diffusely in the batter during cooking. Instead, she came up with a delicious type of cookie that she called Chocolate Crispies.

The cookies became such a hit with both locals and visitors to the inn that she had to purchase chocolate bars in large quantities. Nestle investigated why so many of their chocolate bars were being sold in Whitman, Massachusetts, of all places, and a salesman visited, finding out about the cookies. In 1939 Nestle offered Wakefield a forty-year contract with the company and she accepted. Nestle began selling their chocolate in the form of small pieces that they called "chips," and printed Wakefield's recipe on the bag, which they renamed Toll House Cookies. Thus, an accidental use of chocolate pieces led to a world-famous cookie.

Another food was developed in Philadelphia, where I spent most of my adult life. Pat and Harry Olivieri owned a popular hot dog stand in South Philadelphia during the Depression in the 1930s. They bought the stand at the corner where 9th Street and Wharton and Passyunk Avenues meet. They would always take their lunch break by having a hot dog themselves, but one day Pat grew tired of the same lunch every day and instead bought a pound of thinly sliced beef, which he fried up on the griddle with onions and put in a roll. He had not experimented with this previously. The stand was a favorite of cab drivers in Philadelphia, and that day a cabbie happened to come up to the stand for a hot dog. This was the unexpected event, since it coincided with Pat's manufacture of the first steak sandwich for himself. One look (and smell) of the concoction that Pat came up with convinced the cabbie that he needed to have that sandwich. Pat, being interested in business, had the foresight to sell the sandwich to the cabbie for a dime.

Word quickly spread, and Pat and Harry Olivieri were out of the hot dog business and into the steak sandwich business, opening up Pat's King of Steaks (still there) near their former stand at the corner of 12th Street and Passyunk Avenue. Their sandwiches now have competition from numerous other stands (and almost any other type of American food restaurant) that sell steak sandwiches all over Philadelphia, and indeed, all over the U.S. Cheese (Cheez Whiz for the connoisseur) was added in the 1950s, and you can now add grilled mushrooms, sweet or hot peppers, and condiments. But say "Philadelphia cheesesteak" and anyone in the U.S. will know what you are talking about.

Speaking of food, my own minor food-related serendipity occurred one night when my children were small. I was always an incompetent chef. The first time I started cooking was in medical school when I shared an apartment with a classmate. It was always dry cereal with milk for breakfast, and our dinners included the repertoire of hamburgers, spaghetti with meatballs, Shake 'n Bake chicken, pork, or fish, and Chef Boyardee canned ravioli (I kid you not). The first time Terry came to dinner at my house, Chef Boyardee was served. After we married, Terry did most of the cooking, while I usually stuck to grilling steaks or hamburgers but not much else. Terry stayed home with our three children (her choice) when they were small. But when the youngest was in first grade, she went back to finish her education at Bryn Mawr College.

One day I came home and the kids told me that Terry had called, letting them know she was running an experiment in the lab, would be late, and I was to get dinner for the kids and myself. My immediate reaction was to ask the kids what kind of fast food they wanted, which they (believe it or not) balked at. They also said that ground beef was defrosted and in the refrigerator. I asked them if they wanted hamburgers or spaghetti and meatballs, which they also declined since they had recently had both. Looking in the cookbooks we had, and then in the refrigerator and cupboards, I realized that I had the ingredients to make beef stroganoff. I got the idea that maybe I could cook some fancier dishes that I had never tried before. So the need to feed the kids and myself was an unexpected event, which led to my curiosity about cooking. I went to work, served it, and they loved it. I could cook! And I was hooked. I began by cooking at least two or three nights a week, and after a couple of years was cooking every night. This has continued to the present.

We had a tradition of having a fish dinner and then a movie on Saturday nights. Our kids, impressed with my newfound culinary skill, asked if I could make dinner that Saturday night. Terry wholeheartedly agreed, and I proceeded to go shopping for the ingredients and make flounder Florentine (flounder filets, sour cream, diced sautéed onions, and spinach) that was a big hit. Several weeks later, we would have our usual fish dinner on Saturday night and grilled steaks on Sunday. I again went shopping for ingredients for the flounder Florentine, as well as what I needed for Sunday, including mushrooms to slice and sauté to serve with the steaks. When I got home, I realized I had overdone it with the amount of the mushrooms I bought and thought, *What if I sliced and sautéed some for the Florentine?* I made the flounder dish on Saturday with the sautéed mushrooms added. The kids tasted the dish and, in unison, asked me what I had done. Fearing the worst, I asked them if they didn't like it. Their reply was, "Are you kidding? This is fantastic! What is it?" I named it Flounder Kennett Square (a large mushroom-growing area west of Philadelphia), and it is now famous in our family. I never went outside the family with it, but at least in our own family, a serendipitous food addition has been a hit.

Research Occurrences

I have also had some serendipitous occurrences that have sparked some of my research projects and publications, adding to my career. One that comes to mind occurred when I was the associate chief of the Division of General Internal Medicine at a Veterans Affairs Medical Center in 1996. I had done a number of studies looking at physicians' values involving ethical decisions over the previous ten years. Mark Berger, a hematologist-oncologist, came up to Peter Ubel, another general internist at the VA. Mark asked Peter about helping him with a letter that he wanted to submit to a journal. He'd had an unusual experience in which a patient started getting treatment at the VA from Mark for a type of lymphoma (cancer of the lymph glands). He had just started treatment at the VA, as he was being treated previously at a private hospital. Mark asked him to get his previous records so he could see what treatment had already been given, and he noted that they contained a different name from the patient's. The patient sheepishly admitted to using his cousin's medical insurance in order to obtain care until his own insurance at the VA went through. I looked into this and found that there were no state laws requiring physicians to disclose patient insurance fraud, though physicians cannot be complicit with ongoing insurance fraud. I also found that no one had done any studies about physicians' views on this.

I immediately got the idea that we should use hypothetical scenarios to see what physicians would do if they encountered such occurrences. We developed a survey that we sent to members of the American College of Physicians. It presented multiple scenarios with hypothetical patients, all of whom had previously used a relative's insurance to obtain care. The survey revealed that the physicians were more likely to report these fictitious patients when the patients had an acute illness as compared to a terminal illness, had previously committed insurance fraud, or were wealthy as opposed to poor. In addition, physicians who had actually experienced patients who engaged in insurance fraud were more likely to report the hypothetical patients. This showed that physicians held certain biases in reporting fraud that might affect their decision-making. We presented this paper at the annual meeting of the Society of General Internal Medicine, and it was published in the *Archives of Internal Medicine.* So by paying attention to the story Mark Berger told and thinking about the issue, I was able to publish another study on values and ethical decision-making.

Everyday serendipitous events range from those that have a small impact to those having a profound, even life-saving impact on someone. As to the first, I was at one point beginning to teach others about how to communicate bad news, with one key element being the need to eliminate medical jargon when talking with patients and their families. Jargon is used as a shorthand in medicine but it can be confusing and overwhelming to patients. My challenge was to find a way to introduce what jargon was and how patients *felt* when exposed to it.

I began by looking through texts and couldn't really find a useful way of demonstrating jargon to medical students, residents, and practicing physicians. I then realized, as described by Max Decharne, that jargon changes over time. So if I picked some jargon from a prior point in time not well known to the current general public, I could stump the physicians trying to translate it and have them recognize what patients experience. I hit by chance upon a phrase that was perfect. See if you can understand what

Chapter 2: Everyday Serendipity

I am trying to relate: *There is a bear in a plain wrapper on 5 doing flip-flops, handing out green stamps.*

This is trucker CB slang from the 1970s for "There is a highway patrolman (they wear the Smokey the Bear hats) in an unmarked police car (plain wrapper) on I-5, staying in the median and patrolling both sides of the road (doing flip-flops), handing out speeding tickets (green stamps)." I have used this very successfully ever since in order to demonstrate what jargon is all about, and how we as physicians need to avoid it to help our patients understand the information about their illnesses.

The unexpected events really are a part of our daily lives. For example, the other day I was getting something in the kitchen and happened to notice my car keys on the kitchen table. Now that is unusual, since I *always* keep my keys and wallet on the desk in our bedroom. What were the keys doing in the kitchen? Then I suddenly remembered: I was going to get gas in the car the previous day, when I had a phone call and some other things I needed to attend to that interrupted my plans. I don't like getting gas in the morning or evenings when the lines are long, and since retiring a year ago, I have the luxury of going during the day. So I picked up the keys, got my wallet, and went to the gas station. Now, you might say that it was too simple an event to even mention. But these simple events are just very minor examples of the kinds of things happening to all of us all the time. I have become more acutely aware of them since becoming more self-aware and more interested in the phenomenon of serendipity. But I am sure that if you sat and thought about these kinds of events, you could also generate some stories where an unexpected event led you to something fortuitous.

Since unexpected events are so common, in the coming week see if you can find the small unexpected events in your life—how your recognize them and utilize them. Once you are able to do this on a regular basis, the more meaningful and important unexpected events will also become a recognized part of your life.

Out of Necessity

Often someone will come up with an idea or invention because of need. This may occur when something is expected and the original product, often some type of food, isn't available, or when people are having a difficult time with a product. Then again, sometimes someone may experience an untoward event and want no one else to have to undergo a similar experience.

My story regarding something of benefit because of a specific need involves the teaching of residents in a particular area of communication. We were trying to have internal medicine residents at Christiana Care Health System in Wilmington, Delaware, be better trained and more sensitive when giving bad news. I had an interest in communication, but I was newly interested in the subject of giving bad news because of a horrible experience my wife and I had in 1997. She, like I, had a history of migraines since childhood, so the aura (weird neurologic symptoms that precede the headache in some migraine sufferers) was not unknown to us. Most auras are visual, like flashing lights, a blind spot in the vision, et cetera (though I have had other auras as well).

One night in March of 1997, she awoke and told me that her left arm had been moving uncontrollably for a few minutes, followed by a headache. Symptoms like these in the middle of the night can be a warning that something more serious might be going on. I would have sent a patient of mine with those complaints to get an MRI and to be seen by a neurologist. However, although the doctor that was me knew this was a red flag for a brain tumor, the husband that was me dismissed the symptoms. Yet when they repeated themselves two months later, I had her see a neurologist who also thought it might be just her migraines, but did order the MRI, which she went for the following week. Terry was telephoned by the neurologist after she had the test. He told her that she had something "white in her brain," and referred her to a neurosurgeon. Terry called me at work crying hysterically, with the firm conviction that she had brain cancer.

We went together to see the neurosurgeon, who asked questions, performed a physical examination, and showed us the MRI, talking about the tumor that was present and offering us the option of a biopsy or craniotomy (open surgery to remove as much of the tumor as was possible). When my wife started crying, he just looked on. I was grieving, yet very angry that the surgeon just stood there rather than trying to comfort us. She ended up going through a lot of treatment, surviving, and enjoying a long life afterwards. We actually did become quite close with the neurosurgeon over time. Unfortunately, the experience left both of us scarred.

Because of this negative experience, I was intent on trying to teach others how to relate such news to patients. The problem we had with the residents was that role-playing (one resident playing the role of the patient and the other acting as the physician giving bad news) was really not very helpful when we tried it, since the residents had little experience with loved ones being seriously ill and also may have been somewhat frightened of taking on that role even in a role-play situation. Using standardized patients (actors who are trained to act the role of the patient) involves a complex and costly infrastructure. How could we then get residents to experience the giving of bad news in a safe, experiential way?

When my wife was going through her treatments for the brain cancer, we both attended support groups at the Philadelphia branch of The Wellness Community, a program for those with cancer and their caregivers in many cities across the U.S. My experience was that people with cancer want to share their experience (especially their experiences with physicians) so that others can be appropriately supported. It so happens there is a branch of The Wellness Community in Wilmington, Delaware. It suddenly clicked as a moment of serendipity: I could see if patients at the Delaware branch of The Wellness Community would be willing to help teach residents how to give bad news.

I went there and talked with some of the patients. They were all eager to participate in an educational program where they would perform the role of being a standardized patient using their own stories and illnesses as the scenarios. In other words, they would have their diagnosis told to them once again by a resident playing the role of the physician informing them. At the beginning of the workshop the residents had no idea that the patients really had the diagnosis of cancer, since they had experienced standardized patients as a routine event during medical school. They all assumed that this would be the same type of experience. However, at the end of the workshop, the residents knew these were real patients with cancer from how they acted, and felt it was a profound experience.

involved. Before the 1930s, people had to carry their food and groceries in bags or baskets that they brought to the store. These would become quite heavy if one were buying a large number of items. Sylvan N. Goldman of Oklahoma City owned a supermarket in town, and he was eager to improve the business in his store. He was trying to think of a way of making it more convenient for shoppers to carry the groceries they purchased as they roamed the store. One night in 1936, Goldman was sitting and thinking about the problem when an inspiration came upon him. He realized that if he welded two chairs together, added wheels on the bottom and a basket on top, customers could wheel their goods around the store and would therefore be more likely to buy more items. In addition, the chair he was sitting on was a metal folding chair, and he realized he could fold up the cart as well.

Goldman first put out his folding basket carriers in his store on June 4, 1937. He found that most customers avoided the shopping carts, perhaps believing they might be viewed as weak or inferior. Goldman then came up with an idea to promote the shopping carts: he paid some people to use the carts in the store, acting like they were also shoppers. Soon real shoppers caught on, and eventually the shopping carts were a big hit. Could you imagine *not* using a shopping cart in a store if you were planning on buying a lot of items? They are ubiquitous, with hundreds of millions in use. Again, the need to make things easier in order to increase his business led to a serendipitous invention for Sylvan Goldman that has its application almost universally (at least in the United States) today.

Frustration Can Lead to Success

Opportunities for discovery and change often stem from one's frustration with something in everyday life. Those who listen to the knocking on their door often come up with an answer to the problem they are facing. Medicine has been revolutionized by the use of computers. Everyone knows about robotic surgery, computerized scanning (CAT scans and magnetic resonance imaging, or MRIs), but we now also have electronic health records (EHRs). Along with the use of computers for health records, many institutions have given patients an electronic messaging system, or portal, to communicate with their physicians. However, due to the increase in tasks that physicians, especially primary care physicians, have to do on a daily basis, messages sent by patients may not be seen for up to seventy-two hours after they are sent. We warn patients that they should call us or 911 if they are having acute serious symptoms, but I was noticing that some patients would still instead use the patient portal to communicate such symptoms. This was very concerning to us, since our nurses (who screen our messages and phone calls) would usually respond to phone calls first, with the assumption that they were more pressing.

Upon looking through the literature, we found articles stating that patients universally use patient portals appropriately, meaning only for routine issues and not when having acute symptoms. It seemed like some of these studies may have been biased (as many research studies are; this is not a critique of them but rather what we term *research bias*). We did find one study that indicated that 22% of the patients used the electronic portal to relate symptoms to their physicians. These included all types of symptoms, but even those that may seem innocuous can sometimes be indicative of a more serious problem. For this reason, any messages with symptoms, which may not receive a response in a timely manner if relayed by a patient portal, are inappropriate.

We undertook a study examining what the patients of our own practice at the University of California San Diego Internal Medicine Group would do in hypothetical situations, such as sudden onset of chest or abdominal pain, very high blood pressure, abnormal blood tests and imaging (MRI) tests, et cetera. We found that a significant portion of our patients would be likely to use our electronic portal to send messages about symptoms and abnormalities, even when they were life-threatening (such as acute chest pain indicative of a heart attack), and expected to receive messages through the portal in return. We therefore changed the way we handled our messages, instructing our nurses to scan the messages sent via the electronic portal at least several times a day. In this way, we could avoid a patient having a serious condition that was missed for several hours or days. So the unexpected event of having some patients send messages with serious symptoms instead of calling or going to the ER led me to look at the literature, which contradicted what we were finding in our own practice. This then resulted in the study that we conducted and led to a change in our practice and to a publication in medical literature.

There are also well-documented cases of invention stemming from the inventor's frustration. Take Samuel Morse, who, living in the early 1800s, was used to the frustration of long delays in communication. It often would take weeks or months (depending on the distance and local infrastructure) for letters or messages to get from one person to another. Morse was an artist, educated at Yale College (later Yale University); while there, he attended lectures on electricity. He went on, though, to have a lucrative career in portrait painting. Returning from a stint in Europe, he was on board a ship going from France back to the United States in October of 1832. He was thinking about how long it would take a letter to reach the U.S. from France by traveling on the ship.

Over dinner one night, a conversation ensued about electricity, and how an electromagnet could be created by wrapping coils of insulated wire around a metal rod, with the ends then connected to a battery. When the discussion turned to whether increasing the strength of the magnet by using more coils would slow the current, one of the more astute passengers replied that no matter how many coils there were, and how long the wire, the electricity would flow from one end to the other instantaneously (not exactly true, but for their purposes it was so; electricity, like light, moves at about 186,000 miles per second). Morse was thinking about that, and suddenly realized that if the electricity and electromagnets could somehow be used appropriately, people would be able to communicate with each other instantaneously instead of over weeks or months. This was his moment of recognizing the unexpected event.

Morse decided to give up his artistic career and instead spent all of his time and money developing a method of using electricity to communicate. After many years of experimentation and trial, Morse came up with the telegraph and a code for communicating messages. He succeeded in changing the world by transforming how people communicated.

Doing A Good Deed

Sometimes everyday serendipity occurs in the form of a good deed which occurs accidentally and benefits others. We all know of stories in which someone intentionally does something good for others. We call that altruism. But sometimes altruism may occur accidentally. Though it doesn't directly benefit the individual who comes across the event, it helps others, and that can be tremendously satisfying. My friend Fred Miller, a fellow docent at the San Diego Air & Space Museum, had his own story about this type of serendipity. This involved the forced ditching (landing in water) of a Navy P-3C surveillance anti-submarine patrol plane on duty in the Aleutian Islands. The plane had a runaway propeller that could not be feathered (stopped), and it had already caused two fires in the engine, which were doused by fire retardant. None of the fire retardant was left and the propeller continued out of control. The only option was to ditch the plane in the sub-zero waters of the Arctic Ocean. They were able to get an emergency signal out before going down, and nine of the ten men were able to escape the plane after the ditching, but survival is slim in exposure to that type of climate.

A reconnaissance aircraft was diverted from a strategic mission in order to search for the downed plane. As they approached the location where the plane had gone down, they saw no rafts on the water. They then began a search pattern in enlarging circles, but still had no sighting. The weather was terrible: low clouds, rain, strong winds. It was looking less and less likely that the men would be found. Then suddenly the co-pilot of the reconnaissance jet sighted a flare at two miles ahead, but when they arrived they found no raft. After circling for a while, they caught sight of one of the rafts. Everyone looked in that direction, and the second raft was spotted. When its fuel was low, the reconnaissance jet was relieved by another Navy P-3C aircraft that stayed with the rafts. However, they could not help unless a ship was near.

The P-3C sighted a ship nearby and tried to reach it by radio, blinking lights in Morse code, and again by radio. The ship failed to respond. Just as the P-3C was running low on fuel and ready to depart the area, the ship finally responded. It was a Russian fishing trawler, and they had some difficulty in understanding the situation. They were finally able to make the Russian captain understand, and the men were rescued. Thus, the flare led the reconnaissance plane to the area where the rafts were located, which allowed the rafts to be spotted, and to also locate a trawler nearby which was Russian, but which after some effort was able to understand the situation and save the downed air crew. This was clearly a life-saving sequence of events involving serendipity.

Fred also was directly involved in a serendipitous event that helped others. Fred was a Navy lieutenant and pilot of a P2V Neptune, a particular type of patrol plane which was used for missions like investigating ships and mining harbors, as well as other missions in Southeast Asia at the time of the Vietnam War. A position opened as the base commander of a United States Navy base in Japan. Fred had a great deal of experience in the patrol plane and in Japanese culture, since his wife is Japanese and they spent a lot of time there together. Fred's commanding officer put in a good word for Fred, and he got the position, even though Fred was somewhat junior (most base commanders are at the level of Navy commander or above). But Fred took the job, moved himself and his wife from Vietnam to Japan, and was highly regarded by both the U.S. Navy and the Japanese population on the base.

Chapter 2: Everyday Serendipity

One of the things Fred first noticed was that the U.S. had built structures on the base that were well maintained, but some of the former Japanese structures were in some disrepair. Chief among them was a Shinto shrine. Fred put in a work order with the Japanese workers on the base to do a reconstruction of the shrine, but was told that they couldn't, since it was an annex of the main Shinto shrine in the city, and only certified Shinto shrine workers could attempt the job. Fred then went into the city and asked at the shrine if the annex could be reconstructed for the people on the base. The work was accepted, and the shrine was restored to its former glory. While walking on the base, Fred noticed a pile of wood and rubbish that had been removed from the reconstruction of the shrine. Among them he found a brass lintel from one of the posts in the shrine. There had been two posts, with matching beautiful lintels, but only one was present. Fred assumed that the lintel was going to go into the trash, since as he related, Japanese culture at the time did not treasure old or used materials. He therefore took the lintel to his office, and when he retired shortly thereafter as the last U.S. commander of that base (it was given back to the Japanese), he brought it home to the U.S.

Some years later, Fred was working for a firm in San Diego and was assigned to work in Japan near the base he had commanded. He decided to visit the base, but before doing so, felt it would be a nice gift to give the lintel to the Japanese base commander. Fred's wife was back in the United States visiting with their children and her friends. He had his wife put it in a box and wrap it and bring it with her when she returned to Japan. Fred went to the base and met with the current commander. He was

49

highly honored as the last U.S. base commander but thought that everyone was just being polite.

Fred gave the gift to the Japanese commander who gasped in astonishment when he saw it. He immediately walked quickly to a museum on the base, dragging Fred with him. There in a large glass case stood a depiction of the restoration of the Shinto shrine, and how much it meant to the people of the base. Two posts were in the case, one topped with a twin of the lintel Fred had brought as a gift. The museum depiction and honor of the restoration was now complete. Fred's serendipitous event was one that meant a lot to the people of that Japanese base. Fred received honor and tremendous satisfaction in doing this for the people with whom he had worked. He felt the need to do something special for the Japanese people at the base, since he had a great deal of love and admiration for them given how well they had treated him when he was the base commander. The serendipitous event of giving back the lintel, which was so precious to those people, made the day for him and the people on the base.

Another example is one in which the need occurs in emergencies and leads to the saving of lives and property. In the 1800s firehouses usually had three stories, with the equipment and fire trucks (then pulled by horses) on the first floor, sleeping quarters and a recreational area on the second floor, and a hayloft on the third floor for the horses' hay. There was usually a spiral staircase, which was fairly slow to navigate in the event of a fire call. The third floor stored a binding pole, which was used to secure the hay to the wagon during transportation.

One day in 1878, a fire call came to Chicago's Engine Company No. 21, an all Black firefighting company, and firefighter

Chapter 2: Everyday Serendipity

George Reid was working in the hayloft. He was three floors above and needed to get down to the engine as soon as possible. He grabbed the binding pole and, pushing it vertically into the spiral staircase, slid down to the first floor. Captain David B. Kenyon marveled at the idea, and immediately had a permanent pole installed with a circular area surrounding it to allow access for the firefighters to slide down to the first floor. The pole was three inches in diameter, made from Georgia pine, and was sanded and coated with several coats of varnish and paraffin. It was soon realized that Company No. 21 was always first to appear at any fire, and the chief of the fire department had fire poles installed in all of Chicago's fire companies. Soon, poles were in almost all fire companies in all cities across the United States. Such an innovation helped to save both property and lives due to the increased speed of getting to the location of a fire.

So everyday serendipity, whether it comes from accidental discovery, in response to some need, or in response to some frustration, can significantly change how things are done or help to invent something useful, or be of significant meaning for society, and in turn reward the individual who came up with the idea. But there may also be times when someone consciously works on an idea or solution to a problem, discovering the answer, idea, or product as a consequence. Some call these events *pseudoserendipity*, since the solution or idea presents itself while one is working on the problem, rather than having something occur accidentally. However, often the discovery or solution to the problem does occur in an accidental manner. For that reason, I have included a number of these occurrences in this book, and we shall explore them in the next chapter.

CHAPTER 3
GET YOUR THINKING CAP ON

S o what exactly do I mean by pseudoserendipity? It actually occurs in two flavors. The first are those instances in which someone suggests, leads, coerces, et cetera, someone into an idea or area of discovery which ends up being very fruitful. This can be a change in one's career stemming from the influence of a mentor, for example, or even occasionally a scientific idea or technological development. The end result, and the "aha" moment, still often occur in a serendipitous fashion. The other flavor is when someone is working on a problem or idea for quite a while, and the solution comes to them in a serendipitous way. We will explore both of these types of serendipity.

A Blind Date?

Teachers, mentors, and colleagues can often have a significant impact on an individual's career, and even sometimes help guide the type of work or research that they begin to investigate. I have already discussed how I came to the decision to go into medicine, but the decisions to enter general internal medicine and to perform survey research specifically involving aspects of patient-physician communication were influenced by three of my main mentors early in my career. The University of Pennsylvania had a unique curriculum, with only one year of basic science followed by three years of clinical rotations, with a few months of extra basic science electives. I was a second-year medical student at Penn, on my first inpatient internal medicine rotation in January 1974, when two things affected my decision to do primary care. The first was a fantastic mentor in the persona of the third-year resident on the rotation, John Eisenberg. John would go on to be one of the national leaders in general internal medicine, and he showed me the delights of primary care, especially the opportunity to get to know one's patients.

However, I was still undecided, thinking about perhaps a subspecialty of medicine or pediatrics as my career, since I also had spent two summers in a gastroenterology lab run by a gastroenterologist whom I really admired. Then a negative occurrence helped me make the decision.

Medicine grand rounds consisted of lectures by famous physicians in medicine, as well as lectures by the occasional faculty member. Occasionally an actual patient would be brought in, and the faculty member giving grand rounds would have to determine the diagnosis from the history and physical examination he or she conducted and then discuss the condition. In this case, the patient was someone with aortic stenosis (a severe narrowing of one of the valves of the heart) along with congestive heart failure (damage to the left ventricle, the main pumping chamber of the heart). The faculty member who was giving grand rounds correctly assessed the situation and began to discuss the diagnosis along with the prognosis. At that time, although open-heart surgery with mechanical valve replacements was common in patients who had advanced congestive heart failure as a result of the aortic stenosis, in this case, a valve replacement was not feasible. These patients lived, on average, about six months, and the presenter stated this in no uncertain terms.

At that point the patient at the front of the auditorium became wide-eyed and began to cry, as no one had previously told him this information. The presenter giving grand rounds looked down at the patient with some disdain, then back up at the audience and continued his scholarly lecture.

I was shocked that a physician would not show empathy for the patient. I knew that not all specialists were like this, but it made me realize that a specialist would not usually develop a deep and long-lasting relationship with a patient. This was what I was looking for and decided that I instead wanted to go into a primary care field. Primary care encompasses internal medicine, family medicine, and pediatrics. It is the total, all-encompassing care of the patient, mostly in the outpatient setting, but also when the patient is hospitalized with an acute illness or complication of a chronic illness.

My second mentor was a resident on one of my pediatric electives. At that time, in my third year at Penn, I was sure I wanted to go into an academic career in some form of primary care. I really liked internal medicine, but I thought I also liked pediatrics. At that time there was no residency in medicine-pediatrics; one could do both residencies, although it was a larger investment of time (five or six years instead of three for either medicine or pediatrics alone). Additionally, there were as yet very few faculty positions in medicine-pediatrics, especially in academic medicine. Medicine-pediatrics allows a physician to be trained in the care of adults (internal medicine) as well as those from birth to eighteen years of age. I was therefore in a quandary about what to do, and my pediatrics resident knew this.

One day he saw me playing with a two-year-old girl on the floor, and told me I should go into medicine. I asked him, incredulously, why he didn't like pediatrics. He responded that he absolutely loved pediatrics. I told him I did too, and that was why I was having such a hard time deciding. He responded by telling me that no, I liked playing with kids, not being a pediatrician. I saw the light; there was no way I could do some of the things to kids that I would have to do as a pediatric resident, much less as a pediatrician. I realized that medicine was for me.

My third major experience came when I had started my academic career on the faculty at the University of Connecticut as Assistant Professor of Medicine in the Division of General Internal Medicine. Frank Davidoff, MD, was my division chief, and he was a very wise and skilled mentor. At that time I knew I was interested in medication compliance, or how patients take their medications (we now call it medication adherence to avoid the pejorative terminology). However, I wasn't sure what it was that attracted me to that particular subject.

All faculty in clinical divisions of medicine have four tasks: seeing patients, teaching, university service (otherwise known as committees), and scholarly activity or research. Frank brought me into his office one day and asked me about what I planned to do from a scholarly point of view. I told him about my interest in medication compliance, and he indicated he knew that there were some faculty in the dental school interested in that topic, and offered to introduce me to them. But he didn't leave it at that; Frank then asked me to explain *why* I had the interest that I did. I thought about it and could only say that the thing that interested me most was that the relationship between the physician and the patient had a significant impact on whether the patient takes medication as they are directed. Much research had shown by then that when the patient feels more satisfied with the relationship they have with their physician, they are more likely to take the medication that the physician has prescribed. This also keyed into the feelings I had about wanting to have in-depth relationships with patients. This was at the heart of my wanting to be a physician.

Frank became interested and told me about a group called the Task Force on Doctor and Patient, which was part of the Society for Research and Education in Primary Care Internal Medicine (SREPCIM, now known as the Society for General Internal Medicine, SGIM). He offered to fund my way to the next SREPCIM meeting and to introduce me to the members of the Task Force on Doctor and Patient.

The introductions to the social psychologists at the University of Connecticut, and to SREPCIM and the Task Force on Doctor and Patient members, helped to shape my research and teaching interests for the rest of my career. From the group of social psychologists at the dental school, I learned about survey instruments and survey research, which I have used in approximately sixty different studies over the years. And my interests in patient-physician communication continue to this day, mostly in education but also in some of the research I have conducted.

More recently, someone I was mentoring guided me into an interest I have always had but had not thoroughly explored. Courtney Hanson, MD, was a junior faculty member in our Division of General Internal Medicine at the University of California, San Diego. I was helping her with some research projects, and in August of 2018 she suggested we get some lunch, as we had the afternoon off. We decided to go to the San Diego Air & Space Museum in Balboa Park, as it was close to home for both of us and she knew of my lifelong interest in airplanes and spaceflight. In grade school I built model airplanes and played with toy airplanes. The best birthday present I ever received from my brother was a toy jet fighter cockpit that I played in for hours on end. Then, when we started going into space, I was glued to the TV set almost from launch to splashdown, for Mercury flights in grade school through Gemini and Apollo flights in high school. I felt like I was there when Walter Cronkite broadcast the first moon landing when I was in college. The problem was that I had poor eyesight, bad navigational sense and ability, and mediocre math skills, so a career in the field was not in my future.

We had a nice lunch at the café in the museum, talking about some aspects of her research. After lunch, she suggested I show her some of the artifacts of the museum that I knew about, specifically airplanes in the World War II gallery and spacecraft the museum had. I was showing her around when she headed toward an area where two of the docents were sitting. She looked at them, pointed back to me, and said, "He wants to be a docent." I told her I really didn't want to do that. I felt that I didn't have the time to learn the information required, let alone the time required to actually be a docent. She looked at me and said, "Neil, you will be retiring in a year. Yes you do."

I realized that since I was planning on retiring, I needed to have some outside interests. I told the docents I *did* want to be a docent, started training, and after only three months passed my "check ride" (the requirement was to do fifteen partial tours of the museum, followed by a full tour rated by two senior docents). I started by working two half days per week, and after retirement went to two full days. I have learned something every day I have walked into the museum and have loved every day I have been there. In a way, I became part of the aviation and space community, a dream from childhood fulfilled.

The greatest thrill came in March 2019. We have the original Apollo 9 command module in the museum on loan from NASA, and at that time it was the fiftieth anniversary of the flight. We had a gala in its honor, with the three original astronauts, Jim McDivitt, Rusty Schweikert, and Dave Scott, in attendance, along with Gene Krantz from Mission Control. As docents, we had the honor of talking with them and exploring what it was like to be in space and on the moon. Although Apollo 9 tested out the lunar module in Earth orbit, Dave Scott went on to become the mission commander of Apollo 15, and was the seventh man to walk on the moon.

Another gala in July of 2019 celebrating the fiftieth anniversary of the lunar landing of Apollo 11 also brought Charlie Duke, the lunar module pilot of Apollo 16 and the tenth man to walk on the moon, who I also had the honor of meeting and talking with. All of the astronauts of the era, especially those who actually walked on the moon, were my heroes from childhood and teenage years. It was an incredible thrill to be able to meet them, shake hands with them, and talk with them about their experiences. All were gracious and tolerant of the number of questions I asked them. All of this occurred because someone I was mentoring had the sense to guide me to something I really wanted to do.

Sometimes it takes multiple gentle (or not so gentle) nudges before someone will take advantage of a serendipitous event. By 2005, both of our daughters had moved to San Diego; our older daughter was a medical student at UC San Diego, and our younger daughter was an undergraduate at San Diego State University. She had moved to San Diego after experiencing a very cold winter at Cornell and then visiting her sister, deciding there and then to make the move. Our son, our oldest offspring, was firmly ensconced in a suburb of Chicago. We still lived outside of Philadelphia, and as we got older we began to think that it might make sense to move to a warmer climate and be closer to at least some of the kids.

I started looking at ads in medical journals, but didn't find any promising positions out west. After looking for several months, in the spring of 2006 I found an ad in the *Annals of Internal Medicine* about a position in the Division of General Internal Medicine (my specialty) involving outpatient care, teaching, and research. Since I am an academic general internist, this was perfect, and in fact, the only type of position at an academic medical center in San Diego that I would have considered. I was tremendously excited and began daydreaming about living out in California. Even Terry, born and raised in Philadelphia with all of her family still there, was eager to move. I excitedly sent in my curriculum vitae with a cover letter. The months went by, and I didn't hear a word. I assumed that since I had a great deal of experience and a really good track record, the only reason I would not be considered was because they were only interested in California physicians. I put the idea of moving to San Diego out of my mind. It instead just became our favorite vacation destination.

About six months later I wasn't looking for jobs anymore, as I was perfectly happy on the faculty of Christiana Care Health System in Wilmington, Delaware, doing a lot of teaching and research besides some patient care. I was reading the various scientific articles in the *Annals of Internal Medicine* when the issue I was reading slipped out of my hands and landed on the floor. It opened to the ads, where I saw that UC San Diego was now looking for a clinical medical director at its outpatient location. This was clearly an unexpected event, but this would be the same position as the one I had previously applied to without a response, except that it had some administrative work involved. I was therefore dismissing it as a possibility. But I brought the ad home and showed it to my wife, saying how it was unfair of them to keep putting ads in the journals when all they really wanted was just local physicians. I told her I wasn't going to apply because of that, and she told me she thought I was being judgmental and presumptive, and that I couldn't know what was happening unless I applied. I thought I would show her I was right and she was wrong, and therefore I sent my curriculum vitae and cover letter electronically.

Within the hour I received a phone call from a secretary asking if I could take a call from Joe Ramsdell, MD, the division chief. Joe outlined the position and apologized for not getting back to me on the previous position I had applied for, stating he felt it was too junior for my level but that this position was ideally suited for me. I went out to San Diego and was very excited about the possibilities.

In January of 2007, I flew out again to San Diego to meet some of the more senior administrators. My older daughter picked me up at the airport, and before going to the hotel we drove around some neighborhoods in La Jolla and Carmel Valley, near the university, looking at houses. I was getting cold feet—this was a move across the country to a city we had only visited previously. I expressed my concerns to her and told her that we could look, but there was no way we were really going to make this move. She drove down a road I had not been on before and stopped at the top of a hill with only scrub brush on both sides. I asked if something was wrong, and she told me she had to show me something. We got out of the car, walked twenty-five or thirty feet to the west, and there we were, standing on the top of a cliff, with the beach three hundred feet below us and the Pacific Ocean spread out in front of us, on a warm, sunny, winter day. It was unbelievably gorgeous, and we had no such vistas on the East Coast. Plus, I was there in the middle of January with just a short-sleeved shirt on and was warm. And Terry and I would be close to two of our kids whom we adored. I felt I had reached Nirvana. How could I possibly turn down something like this? I looked at her and asked her how much *I* had to pay the university to make the move. My fears were gone.

I went on to interview with the administrators, and by the end was convinced that this was the job for me. It had the right combination of patient care, mentorship as a leader, researcher, and teacher, both in the clinic and on campus in small group seminars (the latter of which I always wanted but had not had the opportunity to experience before). I was hooked. When Joe Ramsdell called me at the airport on my way out of town to offer me the position, I readily accepted. He told me to take my time, that the written contract would be coming to me in a few weeks, and I could then definitively give an answer. When it came, I told my wife that if I signed, we were committed to moving to San Diego and that it was unlikely that we could move back to Phila-delphia, as I was in my mid-fifties and a job like this would not be likely to come along there. I said that it was her last chance to back out of the deal. She looked at me and said, "I don't care what you do. I'm moving to San Diego." I gleefully signed and we moved a few months later.

Was it the right move? It sure was! I was blissfully happy ful-filling all of the roles at the university. I loved the weather, and my wife and I loved being close to two of our kids. The culmination came when two years later my daughter graduated from UCSD medical school. Since I was on the faculty, I got to march in the graduation and place the hood on her as she went on the stage, which signified her receiving the MD degree. I still get tears in my eyes as I write this.

I cannot say what others' experiences have been, but I clearly had my career (and my enjoyment in retirement) influenced by being gently guided into decisions that were really waiting for me. My experience is that these were serendipitous in that the realization of an interest came to the fore by discussions with a mentor, friend, or daughter, and might not have occurred if my deep-seated interests were not pointed out to me by someone else.

However, once these were pointed out to me, it was up to me to do something productive with them. We will discuss this further in Chapter 5.

A Blind Date For Industry

The previous examples related to some of the moves we made in terms of my career, post-career life, and location, in which I was gently, or not so gently, nudged in order to make a decision. But there are many examples of occurrences in the industrial environment where multiple players were involved in order to generate the final product. Dow Chemical Company had developed a plastic film called perchlorethylene (see Chapter 5) that was sold to the military in World War II. It was used to bind and protect equipment being transported, as it was impermeable to the corrosive effects of seawater. This was critical in order to protect tanks, planes, trucks, et cetera, which had to be shipped in containers in the ships' hold or on deck. These armaments and other vehicles and planes had potential for critically important parts to rust, thereby making them useless. Perchlorethylene helped to prevent this from happening.

After the war, Dow felt that the uses of the film would be limited, and therefore sold the rights to two of its former employees, John Reilly and Ralph Wiley. Reilly and Wiley did not initiate the purchase, but felt that maybe they could make something of this unexpected event. They had curiosity about whether they could do something with it that would make it into a household product, and began work on the substance, creating a thin, clear, and odor-free film. They tested it and found that it could be safely used to help retard spoilage of perishable products in the home.

They established the Saran Wrap Company, named after the daughters of Reilly (Sarah) and Wiley (Ann), and began marketing the product in 1949. It was a huge success, after which the Dow Chemical Company bought the product back and marketed it to millions of homes. Thus, the employees of Dow, experienced in the nature of the product, were led into its production.

A similar occurrence was the development of the portable flashlight. Joshua Cowen developed an idea for a centerpiece for restaurant tables in the 1890s. He created a metal tube, into which he put a battery and attached a lightbulb at one end. This was placed into a flowerpot with flowers, creating a centerpiece to light up tables in dimly lit restaurants. Unfortunately, this idea was never a real success, and Cowen went in another direction that was of more interest to him.

Along came one of Cowen's salesmen, a man named Conrad Hubert, who was interested in the business. He approached Cowen and bought the rights to his invention. This was a serendipitous moment for both Cowen and Hubert. Hubert saw a new application of the device: Since this lit up areas, perhaps it could somehow be made portable. Households could then have a way to look into dark cellars and attics, illuminate the outside at night, or have a backup if the electricity was out, as often occurred in the early days of electrification in both cities and towns. He developed the "light-stick" and started the American Eveready Company, using batteries previously invented by others. Millions of flashlights have been sold since then.

And Cowen? He developed his passion for toy electric trains. He set up a company and began selling the toy trains in 1901. By 1902, he was selling trains all over the United States. His name was Joshua *Lionel* Cowen, and he was the founder and owner of Lionel Trains.

Often someone is led or coerced by others into an idea or discovery that significantly and positively impacts their personal life and/or career. But there are also times, as mentioned at the beginning of this chapter, when someone wrestles with an idea or problem and then has an "aha" moment. We will delve into these events now.

Deep In Thought

Since ancient times, stories abound about a scientist or inventor who is deep in thought about how to resolve a particular issue or problem and suddenly stumbles across the inspiration for the solution. An example of this is the story of how cellophane, the crinkly plastic wrapper, came into being. Jacques Brandenberger, a Swiss engineer who graduated from the University of Bern in 1895, was in a French restaurant when a customer near him knocked over a glass of red wine, ruining the tablecloth. Brandenberger realized that if he could come up with something that would be a barrier to stains, he would have a sought-after product on his hands. He tried a number of different chemicals, all without success, and then thought about the fact that plants are able to contain water in stems and cells via cellulose, a component of plant cell walls. This was the "aha" moment for him, as he decided to experiment with cellulose and its derivatives to see if that would work. At that time, cellulose was in demand as it was used in synthetic fibers such as rayon.

Initially, the result was one that would not be acceptable to most restaurants, as the cloth came out very stiff. However, with curiosity in his favor, Brandenberger noticed that the cellulose could be peeled off, resulting in a clear sheet. Although not impermeable to water as he initially hoped, the cellulose sheet could be made to be impermeable to fats such as oil and grease. It was also flame resistant. In 1920 he patented the sheet as cellophane and used it for wrapping French perfume and in gas masks. He sold the rights to DuPont Chemical Company in 1923, where William Hale Clark, a chemist, added a waterproof substance, creating cellophane as we know it today.

I have had several studies successfully completed and published by thinking through an issue I encountered. One of these occurred shortly after I had published the articles on physician involvement in capital punishment. I began to realize that capital punishment was an extreme situation and that I needed to find some common, everyday situation that would make a physician act in a way that could be harmful to a patient. But then, overt physical harm would not only be highly unethical, but criminally problematic as well. No physician who adhered to the ethical tenets of medicine would engage in that kind of harm to a patient, no matter what the patient had done.

So how else might a physician cause intentional psychological harm or medical harm to a patient? After thinking about this for quite a while, I thought, what would I do if I had a patient who was verbally abusive to myself and/or the staff? I remembered one such patient I had who had a severe psychiatric illness (she had borderline personality disorder) and would often come to the office berating the staff and myself. It got to the point that the staff pleaded with me to discharge her from the practice. I was torn, as the patient clearly needed medical and psychiatric care, but it was becoming difficult for the staff and the other patients in the waiting room due to her acting out. I finally felt I had to discharge her from the practice after researching under what circumstances it was acceptable for a physician to discharge the patient (that is, when the patient-physician relationship is no longer therapeutic for the patient, or when there is a clear threat to the physician or staff) and how to do so. Our relationship was no longer therapeutic for her and she was verbally abusive, and therefore fit the guidelines. She eventually went to another practice; I was made aware of it when they requested her records. But I never found out what happened to her after that. I don't know if she was harmed by her discharge from the practice, but she was upset that I had done so despite my explanations to her.

Back to my issue with the study; I thought, do all physicians follow these ethical guidelines? I found that no other studies on this issue had been published, just some anecdotal and opinion papers, and had the next study I wanted to do.

I decided to find out how likely physicians were to discharge patients from their practice, with the variable being the type of activity the patient engaged in that might lead to discharge. In that way, we could investigate the bias physicians had toward patients who were not "ideal." We developed a questionnaire with twelve hypothetical scenarios ranging from those that were benign and not warranting a discharge from a physician's practice (e.g., the patient questioning the physician's treatment, non-adherence with the patient's medications) all the way to those where discharge from a medical practice was clearly justified (violent threats by the patient, extreme verbal abuse). The physicians in the study were asked to indicate how likely they were to discharge such patients from their practice for each scenario. We sent the survey to randomly selected primary care physicians in the U.S.

What we found startled us: almost all physicians would discharge patients who verbally abused the physicians or staff, engaged in violent threats, and illegally used narcotics. These situations are understandable and are appropriate reasons for discharging a patient from a practice. However, almost 50% of physicians would discharge patients who failed to provide previous medical records, asked for inappropriate work excuses, or missed appointments frequently. Even more surprising was a small percent of physicians who would discharge patients for medication non-adherence, questioning the physician's decisions regarding medical treatment, or engaging in medical malpractice suits against a previous physician the patient had seen.

Was it that physicians didn't understand the conduct that was ethical in discharging patients, or was it that they didn't care? We did not find out the answer to this question. However, we did ask the physicians why they actually discharged patients from their practices, and their stated occurrences matched how they answered the hypothetical scenarios, lending credence to the fact that they either did not understand the ethical issues involved or did not concern themselves with them. This study was important, and it was published in the *Archives of Internal Medicine*. We also published a series of guidelines on who to discharge from medical practices and how to do so for the *Annals of Internal Medicine*.

Around the same time, I was looking to expand some of the work I had done on physicians' decisions on breaching confidentiality. There is an ethical obligation to maintain the confidentiality of what any patient reports to the physician, *except* when there is a clear present or future risk to one or more other individuals. Thus, physicians would need to maintain the confidentiality about a crime their patient committed in the past. However, the physician would conversely have the obligation of informing both the police and the intended victim of a planned violent crime in the future.

I suddenly had an "aha" moment that led to a serendipitous outcome: one area we had not previously explored was the relationships among physicians and how confidentiality comes into play in those situations. Upon thinking about it, the most obvious issue was one in which a physician displays evidence of impairment. In this situation, if another physician, who is a physician colleague not treating the impaired doctor is aware of the impairment, it is that physician's obligation to report the impaired physician due to the risk of mistakes in judgment or procedures that can cause harm to patients. However, the literature also noted that most physicians are reluctant to inform on their colleagues due to the stigma involved for the impaired physician, as well as for themselves.

The impaired physician is an issue that has gained public awareness, though physicians are still very reticent to inform about a fellow physician. However, most states now have physician wellness programs for impaired physicians without the involvement of the state medical board. Thus, physicians can get the help they need, with rehabilitation in many cases allowing the physician to return to the practice of medicine. But I began to theorize that physicians might be more prone to inform on a fellow physician depending on the type of the impairment. For example, certainly substance abuse of alcohol, cocaine, narcotics, or others is condemned by almost all physicians, but what about the problem of anger management or child pornography for a pediatrician? We therefore decided to look at this issue using hypothetical scenarios in order to get a better sample and protect both informing physicians and possibly impaired colleagues.

We developed a survey with ten hypothetical scenarios of impaired physicians, with five involving substance abuse (alcohol, cocaine, methamphetamine, narcotics, and marijuana) and five involving cognitive or psychological impairment (suicidal thoughts, child pornography, gambling, anger management, and nicotine addiction in a surgeon, interfering with his surgery). One thousand physicians of all different specialties received the survey, with almost half returning the questionnaire. A majority of physicians would report fellow physicians who were abusing the various substances examined in the scenarios, but significantly fewer would report colleagues for the cognitive and psychological issues that we studied. We also found that only 39% of physicians knew of any guidelines on reporting impaired colleagues, and that those who did know about them were more likely to report the hypothetical impaired physicians than those who did not know of such guidelines. We therefore assisted in the medical profession's recognition that physicians needed education and support in the reporting of impaired physician colleagues. We investigated this when we suddenly realized that we could look at breaching confidentiality when it involved physicians on both sides of the ledger.

At one point, I wanted to merge my interests in patient-physician communication with those involving various topics in medical ethics. It is said that communication is the main avenue to resolving ethical issues. But could there be instances of communication problems that lead to ethical issues? I tried to come up with some and could not, other than those involving the research I had already done on breaching confidentiality. I wondered whether there was some other avenue to explore.

When I was at Christiana Care Health System in Wilmington, Delaware, from 1997 to 2007, I was involved in both the ethics committee and a palliative care service due to my interest in communication between the patient, their family, and the physician. This interest also stemmed from my wife's diagnosis of brain cancer shortly before I started work at Christiana Care. Those experiences focused my attention on communication and some ethical issues involving life-threatening illnesses. Several of the physicians we encountered while on the ethics committee and palliative care service had mentioned their attitudes about discontinuation of life-sustaining treatment as requested by the patient. The physicians indicated they would be uncomfortable with agreeing to the patients' wishes. Upon reviewing the literature, I found only a few papers that had addressed this issue, and I realized (an "aha" moment) that a survey was needed to see how physicians would act in these circumstances.

Because of these statements by physicians and the opportunity to investigate the interface between patient-physician communication and medical ethics, we developed a questionnaire using hypothetical scenarios in which patients had various factors that might influence physicians' decisions to either withhold or discontinue four types of life-sustaining treatment: ventilators (breathing machines), feeding tubes, hemodialysis (artificial kidney machines), and use of intravenous antibiotics. We chose these variables due to their varying degree of invasiveness and whether they were considered intensive interventions (ventilators and hemodialysis) or "usual care" (feeding tubes and intravenous antibiotics). Patients in the scenarios were either alert or had dementia, and they were either quadriplegic due to an injury or had a terminal illness. These challenged the physicians regarding their psychological predilection to withhold or withdraw these interventions; we hypothesized it would be easier for physicians to withhold or withdraw treatments in patients who were terminally ill than in those who were simply non-mobile due to quadriplegia, and might also make these decisions in patients with dementia rather than those who were alert, contrary to what one would usually expect. We indicated that the theoretical patients were not depressed and that they had at the time or previously clearly expressed their wishes to withhold or withdraw all of these treatments.

In all such cases, the requests of a patient, as long as they are not depressed and have clearly made their wishes known to the physician or to family members, need to be enacted. Yet, we found that many physicians we surveyed were unwilling to either withhold or withdraw treatment in the scenarios. The results were interesting: As was found in other papers, physicians were less likely to withdraw than withhold any types of medical treatment. Ethics aside, the psychology of withdrawing treatment leading to the death of the patient is often difficult for many physicians despite the fact that both legally and ethically the actions are considered equal and appropriate for patient (not physician) decision-making. However, most startling to us was the fact that physicians were more likely to withhold or withdraw medical treatment from a demented patient who had previously expressed their wishes to a family member than someone who was quadriplegic and could express their wishes directly to the physician. This may be a result of unconscious bias on the part of the physicians. This emphasized the fact that physicians may not always be willing to accede to their patients' wishes and gave us an opportunity to discuss the importance of doing so.

Thinking about various topics and ideas can therefore often lead to something productive. It may not exactly be what some call serendipity, but the "aha" moment may occur while one is pondering the issues at hand. In these examples, the "aha" moment came when I thought about that abusive patient with borderline personality disorder, leading to the study on discharging patients, the thinking about physicians being on both sides of the coin in breaching confidentiality about impaired physicians, and the physicians talking about their discomfort leading to their decisions to withhold and discontinue life-saving treatments. These can often prove valuable to the individual, as well as to others.

Perhaps the most famous example documented in the literature of the "aha" moment involves Archimedes of the ancient Greek city Syracuse. He discovered the idea of the displacement of water as a way of measuring the volume of a complex object. Simple objects, like round balls or other spheres, boxes, cones, et cetera, all have formulas that would determine the volume inside the solid object. But how could you determine the volume of something complex without ruining it? King Heron II of Syracuse was suspicious of a goldsmith who had created a crown of pure gold he had ordered. The king thought the crown felt somewhat lighter than it should, and he felt the goldsmith might have cheated him by mixing in silver or another cheaper metal. The king tasked Archimedes with finding out if this was so without ruining the crown.

Archimedes thought about the problem. He knew that silver and other metals were less dense than gold, and that he could determine the weight of the crown and an equal amount of gold that should have gone into the crown by determining its volume, but he could not figure out how to determine its volume without melting it down since it was not a simple solid object. Archimedes pondered the problem for days on end, sometimes even forgetting to eat, he was so absorbed in the issue. He did go to the public baths one day and happened to notice that the water rose when he stepped in. He suddenly realized that this was the solution to the problem. The amount of water displaced was equal to the volume of his body. He ran out of the baths, shouting the now-famous word, "Eureka!" (I have found it.)

Archimedes went home and filled a bowl to the brim with water and placed it on a pan. He put the crown into the bowl, and water sloshed over the side. Upon measuring the water, he was able to measure the volume of the crown. After weighing the crown and an equal amount of gold that should have gone into it, he found that the crown weighed less, indicating that it had been made of gold mixed with some cheaper silver or other metal. Archimedes was heralded for discovering the truth, and the goldsmith was punished.

We have seen through these examples how chance occurrences (like Percy Spencer's chocolate bar melting in his pocket, leading to the invention of the microwave oven) can open doors. How random events like my being introduced to the social psychologists at the University of Connecticut and the members of the Task Force on Doctor and Patient can change your path. And how deep thought (like Archimedes thinking about how to measure the volume of an irregular object) can broaden your horizons. So how does one become open to those moments and then take advantage of them, turning an observation or idea into a real, productive discovery? I shall explore how others have done this in the next part of the book.

PART II

Set:
Recognizing Serendipity

There are three things that one must do to be successful when turning a serendipitous moment into a productive idea or product: first, recognize that what is occurring has a useful potential; second, work with the idea or process to make it come to fruition; and third, know when to give up on an endeavor that was discovered serendipitously and how to do so.

The first thing one must do is be ready when that unexpected moment occurs. The skills that are needed include self-awareness and a sense of optimism, that is, the belief that serendipitous moments are happening frequently to all of us. Then one must have observational skills to recognize the sight or conversation that needs exploration. The process continues with a sense of curiosity and being able to make connections to previous learning and experiences. Working with the idea or process then requires conscientiousness and persistence, sometimes even in the face of adversity. And the final requirement is knowing when the idea either just isn't going to work, things have changed to make it not be beneficial, or you have decided to move on. At that point one needs to know what to do with the idea, career change, or actual product, and get out and have the resilience to start the process over again. In this second part of the book we shall see how to recognize when an unexpected fortuitous event has occurred.

CHAPTER 4
BEING OPEN TO IT

In this chapter, we will discuss how you must not only have your eyes open to observe the unexpected when it happens, but also an open mind to the possibility of unexpected events. This must be true not only when a sudden event comes along, but also when you have a goal in mind and need to perform and enjoy the small tasks along the way, looking for those unexpected events as they occur. Sometimes during times of adversity, keeping an open mind can help you recognize that the adversity itself, or some aspect of it, is the unexpected event that can be turned into one that is serendipitous and beneficial in some way.

Donald Johnson was a paleoanthropologist (a scientist who investigates the fossil origins of human existence) and an Associate Professor of Anthropology at Case Western Reserve University who had spent almost a month in a desert region of Ethiopia in 1974 searching for evidence of early human life. He had only found animal bones, with no real finds to speak of. The morning of

November 30 of that year, he was readying to leave Ethiopia. He was encouraged by a graduate student to search one more time in the area to see if he could find something of substance.

As it happened, a rainstorm the night before had caused a flash flood, scouring away much of the top layer of sand in the area. He was walking in the gully formed from the morning flood, without seeing anything of significance. Suddenly, something he saw out of the corner of his eye excited him: a fossilized human arm bone. He then noticed lots of other bones and fragments of very old fossilized human remains. He told his colleagues, and they stayed in the region for three more weeks, excavating the site and finding dozens of bones. All were part of a human female who had lived millions of years ago, whom the team named Lucy. This was one of the earliest humans, and she led to new information about our ancestors and how we evolved.

Open Your Eyes

I bring up this incident to make the first point in how to take advantage of serendipitous events. You have to have your eyes open to recognize unexpected events. Johnson's discovery was only possible because of his acute observational skills. Although he had no idea something momentous was going to come of his observations, he was still focused on his work. Donald Johnson had his eyes open that morning when he spied a bone in an area he had thoroughly searched previously. But he also knew that the top layer of soil had been washed away by the flood, and therefore he was carefully exploring one more time when he found the bone that he knew was human but extremely old. This is often true for research of various types, anthropology and archeology dig sites, et cetera. But even in everyday events you need to keep your eyes open, or a serendipitous event may pass you by.

Why do some people overlook important things that others may see? I had insight into this on a trip to Arches National Park in the southeast corner of Utah. This was at the beginning of November, 2019 so the park was a lot quieter than it usually is during the peak season from May through October. I had plenty of space to park the car near the trailheads, and I could therefore leisurely hike the various trails to the spectacular arches and other rock formations. I allowed myself a full day and a half for Arches. I was able to really soak up the beauty that I saw. But as I slowly walked the trails, taking in all of the sights, some hikers power walked past me as though they were on some kind of mission to hike the park in a record amount of time. I commented on this to another visitor, who told me the ranger informed her how long the average day visitor spends in the park. These are visitors not camping overnight; I too was one of the day visitors, staying in a hotel nearby. Keep in mind that there are over eighteen miles of paved roads in a park of almost 120 square miles that has over 2,000 arches. The answer shocked me: on average, about two hours. That would allow someone to drive the length of the park and get out of their car a few times to see things near the road, but not enough time to see some of the more spectacular sights in the park. I am not critical of them; some people might not have had long to spend there. But you certainly miss a lot when you can't spend the time necessary. So it is with other things in life. If you have little time to be observant, you are going to miss some things that might herald a serendipitous event.

Another reason why some people overlook things is because they are so focused on the big picture they tend not to notice the fine details around them that can sometimes be as important, or even more important, than the larger image they are seeing. As I hiked in Arches National Park, I came to one arch named South Window on the Windows Trail. It is a very beautiful large arch, and in fact, is one of the larger arches in the park, and one that you can walk through. Most people stop and look at the arch, then go through to the other side for a different perspective. I happened to stop for a while and take in the amazing vista that I beheld.

I looked to the right of the arch at a prominent rock. As I looked at it, suddenly I noticed that the cracks in the rock clearly formed the appearance of the face of a scowling man. I was amused by this, as none of the guidebooks I had read mentioned anything about it. When I asked a park ranger about it, he said that no one had ever mentioned it to him, and he would have to check it out the next time he was on the trails. The arch itself overwhelms most folks, so the face is almost hidden from view. Oftentimes, what one is expecting (something which is important in diagnosing patients, for example, as in the book by Jerome Groopman, *How Doctors Think*) can influence our observations. I have included a photo of the rock with what I interpreted as the face of a scowling man on the next page.

I must say that I am not nearly perfect in trying to be more aware. In Canyonlands National Park at Grand View Overlook, which is an amazing vista, I was looking around and noticed that the canyons below took the shape of a dinosaur footprint. I had seen this mentioned in a guidebook, but thought I was really hot stuff when I mentioned it to the others around me and got noticed

for it. Then someone else alongside me mentioned "that little crit-ter" near us. Right at our feet on the ledge was a little ground squirrel that I had missed. One can always stop and try to be more aware of one's surroundings.

Many individuals have the gift of keeping their eyes open and discovering wonderful things. In 1940, though much of France was under German occupation, a small village named Montignac in the Lascaux region was in a free zone. There had always been rumors about a cave in the area that had been covered up by workers after the First World War to prevent any accidents. However, four teenagers in the region, led by Marcel Ravidat, a seventeen-year-old, decided to explore the area to see if they could locate the cave. They found the hole, but as they did so, Ravidat's dog fell inside. They widened the hole and were able to save the dog. Intrigued, Ravidat returned several days later with another group of friends and some serious exploring equipment. He was lowered into the cave by a rope, and upon wandering into a side passage saw by his flashlight that the walls were covered with drawings of animals. These were the first prehistoric cave paintings to be discovered and researched by various experts in the field. If not for Ravidat keeping his eyes open and being curious upon the unexpected event of his dog falling into a hole, he, and therefore the world, might never have discovered the prehistoric cave paintings of Lascaux.

Open Your Mind

Having your eyes open can be important in taking advantage of an opportunity, but it is not enough. I believe that having an open mind, and taking risks at times, can be even more important. I was a senior in college in 1971, beginning to apply to medical schools. I had done well and believed I was going to get into a fairly good school, but the top-rated schools were probably beyond my league (as an example, I was eventually rejected by University of Rochester, then a top-tier school). My family was also poor (more about that later), and since I came from New York State, there was a program the state had. If you went to a medical school in New York State, did your residency in New York State, and agreed to practice in the state, your medical school tuition was covered by a state scholarship. I therefore applied to only New York State medical schools.

A friend of mine in college came up to me one day and asked if I was applying to the University of Pennsylvania. I told him I wasn't because of my financial situation, as well as the fact that Penn was out of my reach. He had a better grade point average and better MCAT (Medical College Admission Test) scores than me, so he was more competitive for a school like Penn. Yet he kept on insisting that I should apply. I finally got out of him that he figured he would get an interview there and didn't want to go alone. I could have just declined, but something told me I should go ahead and apply. Maybe it was a desire to please, but also perhaps the idea of keeping an open mind. So I applied, and we both got interviews at Penn.

We drove to Philadelphia from Lancaster, PA (where our college, Franklin and Marshall, was located). The dean told us about how Penn was a cooperative rather than competitive environment (everyone got good residencies because of its reputation, and it was a completely pass/fail system of grading), its unique curriculum (one year of basic science unlike most medical schools with two years, so that Penn had significantly more clinical time), and that Penn had the resources to ensure that money was not an issue. I was suddenly finding myself drawn to Penn. But how would I ever get in?

I was interviewed for admission by one of the psychiatry professors on the admissions committee. I was intimidated, but I felt that I could still present myself well. That is, until he asked me if I knew of a group called Pentangle (I was actively involved in our college radio station, with a morning show and the news department). I told him I didn't, and he promptly told me how good their music was "especially when you are stoned." How should I answer *that*? If I said I didn't do drugs, and he did, he might vote not to accept me for "not being cool enough." If, however, it was a trap, and I said that sounded cool, he would rule against me, as he might not want drugheads at Penn. So I just said, "That's interesting."

At the end of the interview, he commented that I "didn't talk much, but what I said was *so* interesting." I figured that my chances of getting into Penn went from few to zero (I suspected they let him interview but clearly did not let him influence the admission decisions). Sure enough, the following Friday a thin letter from Penn was in my mailbox. Imagine my surprise when I read "Welcome to Penn!" My career and life took an unexpected and wonderful turn because I'd had an open mind. After all, I would not have met the love of my life, my wife Terry, if I had not agreed to explore the possibility of medical school at Penn. I would not be going to Philadelphia on the train in July 1975, as I would have been in a New York State medical school.

This is one of the more important skills that led me to serendipitous events. I already told you the amazing story of how my wife of forty-four years (at the time of this writing) and I met. But one of the possible outcomes of the occurrence could have been that we never got together. When I sat down in my seat on that train, I was very wet, tired, and had come off of a breakup with someone else. When I first heard a conversation up ahead, I was bound and determined to stay out of it and mind my own business. But I kept an open mind and bravely inserted myself in the discussion. The outcome was meeting the most fabulous woman I have ever met.

I have had other incidents in my life which having an open mind led me to something productive or pleasant. When Courtney Hanson led me to the docents sitting at the San Diego Air & Space Museum and indicated I wanted to be a docent, I told her that I, in fact, did not wish to do so. When she said that I should, I decided to keep an open mind and think about the positives and negatives of becoming a docent. At that point I was struck with the idea of doing so. But what if I didn't have an open mind? I might have said sure and then thrown out the book we studied from to become a docent, never setting foot in the museum again, and losing an opportunity that has brought unbelievable fulfillment in my retirement.

Another opportunity presented itself to me as I was preparing to retire. When our family attorney found that I didn't have a financial advisor, he referred me to one. This occurred several years ago. As I was preparing for retirement, I was asked by the financial advisor how I was going to occupy my time, and I told him that I wasn't sure. He knew of my interest in communication skills between physicians and patients, and he said that he had a client who worked for a firm doing something like that and offered to give me her name. I gratefully accepted, and then looked up one of the firms she worked for. It turned out that she utilized surveys for large health care concerns, examining patient satisfaction with their medical care and care given by the physician, which impacts their likelihood of taking medication and also whether they would seek alternative physicians or medical centers. They also did surveys on physician satisfaction with their work environment, as physician dissatisfaction can be costly when a physician decides to move to a different practice. I was somewhat interested in that area, but I couldn't see myself spending a great deal of time in the field. So when she emailed me about another opportunity involving a firm she also worked for, the SullivanLuallin Group here in San Diego, I considered not responding or telling her that it wasn't really something I was interested in. Luckily, I kept an open mind and looked up the firm. They specialized not only in surveys, but also in shadowing and training physicians in communication skills. This was definitely my interest! Since I kept an open mind, I found a company that teaches and investigates areas of my interest as well. Tom Jeffrey, the CEO, and I met by phone and in several meetings among the other physicians and staff in the firm to begin to develop some teaching and other means of helping to treat and prevent burnout in physicians. This has been a tremendously rewarding experience.

Keeping an open mind has also allowed me to take advantage of a number of research opportunities right from the beginning of my career. I have explored some of these through this book, but one important one was when I was looking for an opportunity to connect with and help one of my daughters. At that time she was a third-year medical student at the University of California, San Diego, the year after my wife and I moved there from Philadelphia. I wanted to help her with some research, as she was interested in medical ethics as I was. As a third-year medical student, having presentations at national meetings or publications of scientific articles can help when it is time to apply for residency programs. She was eager to have something in this area, since the time required for this type of research is not long and she would be applying for residencies in less than a year. She sought my help, as I was experienced. But what could we do that would be appropriate for medical students?

One night my wife and I were watching TV, and a commercial came on for an herbal supplement. A guy in a short white coat, stating he was a medical student, was promoting the product. I have some qualms about these advertisements, as many of these products have not been rigorously researched. Physicians are taught to practice by using an evidence-based approach, testing in controlled situations with two populations of subjects: one group that gets the product or medication, and another group that gets a look-alike placebo. There is a code which determines who gets the drug or placebo, and this code is unknown by both the subjects and the researchers. So then, why would a medical student be willing to promote a product without such testing, and how many would be willing to do so?

I considered doing some research to find out, but realized there might be difficulties getting the students to respond given their time constraints and the fact that third- and fourth-year students rarely come together as a group since they are off on clinical rotations. Rather than just looking for something else, I talked to my daughter about the idea and she became very interested. In having an open mind, I realized that we had a project we could do together. I knew that the school had particular pride in the fact that one of their medical students had a father who was on the faculty.

They encouraged collaboration between students and faculty members in general, but especially when they had a relationship.

We went to Jess Mandel, MD, dean of students for the medical school, who discussed the idea with us and graciously allowed us to survey the medical students at UCSD. He was eager to have us collaborating on the project. We developed a survey instrument that included twelve hypothetical products that the students might be asked to promote on television. I have frequently seen practicing physicians and residents promoting products on TV in nationwide ads, and even (albeit infrequently) seen a medical student doing so. The scenarios were grouped by three factors: high risk of the product versus low risk, FDA-approved or not FDA-approved, and remuneration of $10,000, $50,000, or $100,000 for the promotion. We also asked the students the usual characteristics such as age and year of school, but also asked whether they knew of any guidelines on television promotion for drugs or other medicinal products, and the amount of debt they expect to have when they graduated medical school.

Some important findings came out of this study. More than 60% of students were willing to promote medications that were of low risk and were FDA-approved. This is in direct conflict with the American Medical Association position that physicians, trainees, and medical students should refrain from any promotional activities unless they are public service announcements. And even though it was a small percent, some medical students were willing to engage in promotional activities with high-risk, FDA-approved medications or low-risk, non-FDA approved herbal supplements. A few students were willing to promote high-risk, non-FDA approved herbal supplements in clear contradiction to AMA and

Chapter 4: Being Open to It

If you are a committed astronaut, your duty is to support all of the missions in any way you can, but your ultimate goal is to somehow get back into space as many times as possible. A third space flight, in Hadfield's estimation, was highly unlikely. So what did he do at this juncture? He decided he wanted to be as ready as he could be should the unlikely occur. From 2006 to 2008 he was the Chief of International Space Station Operations in the NASA Astronaut Office. In this position, Hadfield was responsible for all of the selection, training, support, recovery (landing back on Earth), and rehabilitation (astronauts on the ISS have a number of adaptations needed when they return from prolonged exposure to weightlessness) of all ISS crew members. He loved the job, but also had really good preparation for another mission on the ISS since he had to interact with space agencies in other countries whose astronauts and cosmonauts were now on the ISS along with U.S. astronauts, and he obtained detailed knowledge of the operations of the ISS.

On December 19, 2012, Hadfield went back to space as the *commander* of the ISS, staying in orbit for 146 days. He had done everything he could to become an astronaut, including joining the Canadian Air Force, applying to and being accepted into test pilot school, and being a test pilot before applying for entry into the astronaut corps. And once he was there, he eagerly and actively participated in every duty and task asked of him, eventually getting into space three times.

I mention all of this to demonstrate how if you are really prepared in your area of expertise or interest, you can recognize an opportunity when it occurs and be ready to take advantage of it. Keeping your eyes and mind open to various possibilities can, in the end, lead to a fruitful experience or idea. The challenge is to stay interested even when you may not be progressing toward a specific goal. However, as Chris Hadfield says, he "got real fulfillment and pleasure from small victories." He did get into space, which few ever achieve. But he also really enjoyed the little things, the work itself, that went into eventually getting there. His mantra was "Be ready. Work hard. Enjoy it!" If you only focus on a major goal, with the expectation that it will occur, you might end up being frustrated, unhappy, and perhaps even unsuccessful. In addition to being ready for the right moment, it is important to enjoy what else you are doing at the time. If you only focus on the important events, you may eventually burn out and miss the opportunity when it comes. The old adage, "Life is about the journey, not the destination," is really true.

Lucky for me, one event occurred that set me on the right track before one of my serendipitous events. I mentioned earlier that I fell in love with teaching when I was exposed to it at Red Letter Day at my small rural high school. But teaching involves appearing before a group of people in order to impart some knowledge to them. Why was it that I found it so enjoyable when I tried it?

I think that an event four years before set me on the course I later followed. One day, when I was a freshman in high school, a friend and I were looking at the school's events on a board and saw posted a call for auditions for the fall play, *Our Town* by Thornton Wilder. He dared me to try out. I had no interest, but a ninth grader can never turn down a dare. I kept an open mind as to the possibility of being involved in the theater at school. So I tried out and got the part of Wally Webb, a non-speaking part. I was hooked, and from then on I tried out for every fall and spring play in our school. Mind you, I was *not* a very good actor, and usually if I got a role at all it was a small part. But I was there at every tryout, every rehearsal, and every performance of every play for four years. Why? Because first of all, I loved being involved in all aspects of the theater, from making posters to practicing lines as a stand-in. Second, I never knew if someone would drop out and the part would be given to me. And third, I gained comfort and confidence in front of an audience. So no, I never became an actor, but I did eventually become a confident and talented teacher of medicine. After all, teaching is in some ways like being on stage, which I loved. By looking to the little things and finding enjoyment in them, and keeping an open mind about it, I was able to convert that opportunity into something very fruitful in my career.

Let me then address the last point in this chapter, one that we usually don't like to talk about. It is also important to be observant and keep an open mind when something untoward has happened in your life or career. We will talk more about this in Chapter 6. However, I do want to share one personal story about keeping an open mind during adversity, since it led to my co-authoring a paper that was published in the *Annals of Internal Medicine*, a prestigious journal.

After my wife, Terry, had surgery for the brain cancer that she was diagnosed with in May 1997, the plan was to go forward with radiation treatments that summer, and then in the autumn start adjuvant chemotherapy. The chemotherapy was given even though the tumor was completely removed and also treated with radiation treatments. This was in case any individual tumor cells had broken loose and traveled to other parts of the brain or spinal cord. She tolerated the radiation treatments well except for fatigue and had medication for the slight amount of nausea she had. It was a tough time for her and an emotionally difficult time for me. But she was doing well by the third month of the chemotherapy. We decided to take our family on a Christmas trip to Scottsdale, Arizona. Terry and I felt we all needed a break from everything, and she felt able to handle it. She had actually gone back to playing some tennis before we left for the trip, which I booked.

A week before the trip, Terry had a follow-up MRI of the brain to assess the response to her treatment. She was to see her neurosurgeon after we got back from Arizona. Being confident that everything was good since she was doing well, I decided to call the radiology department in order to get the results. I figured I could get the news and therefore reassure everyone that everything was fine before we went on the trip. I was informed instead that the tumor had regrown despite the treatment, a very bad prognostic sign. I was devastated and was thinking that this would be the last trip we went on together as a family. I wanted to spare everyone the news while on vacation and kept the news to myself. I had to suffer alone, which was one of the hardest things I have ever done.

While on the trip, in a beautiful hotel at the foot of Camelback Mountain, I would often go off by myself on the trails in order to cry and not have everyone observe it. But the kids knew anyway; years later they said I was not acting normally during the trip. So everyone had a less than happy time, except for Terry, who actually loved the vacation. As it turned out, she then underwent stereotactic radiosurgery after we returned from the trip, and had to have a second surgery the following October, but has been cancer-free ever since.

Chapter 4: Being Open to It

In the years after the trip, I did open up to Terry and told her that I knew the results of the MRI but kept it from everyone. She was upset, not because I had hidden the information, but that I had subjected myself to that agony instead of just waiting and letting the neurosurgeon tell us at the appointment we had when we returned. Her concern was for me.

It was a very stressful time for all of us, perhaps especially for me in knowing the information but having to hide it from everyone, and a sobering experience since I had acted in some ways as my wife's physician. I actively sought out the information rather than having her neurosurgeon inform us. I happened to attend a workshop at the Society of General Internal Medicine a few years later in which Erik Fromme, MD, Stewart Babbott, MD, and Brent Beasley, MD, talked about the conflict physicians have when they act as a physician for a loved one. The workshop intrigued me; my curiosity and privilege as a doctor allowed me things others without an MD degree wouldn't have. This was exactly what the workshop was about. This was an unexpected event, and I knew we could do something important with it. I kept an open mind about it, as I knew I would be exposing my vulnerability in such a subject and writing about it for a major medical journal.

At the end of the workshop, rather than just walking out of the meeting, I told Erik, Stewart, and Brent that we needed to write a paper about our experiences. We chatted and decided that we would need to be honest about our experiences, which I felt might be cathartic. The paper was written, and I came up with the general guideline that physicians should do for their loved ones who were ill only what someone without an MD or DO

(Doctor of Osteopathy) could: generally helping to explain the medical facts, suggesting a physician the loved one should see, providing education, et cetera. Physicians, we decided, needed to avoid things like writing prescriptions for loved ones, diagnosing their medical problems, ordering tests, and yes, finding out results of their tests from the laboratory or radiology as I had done. As I mentioned, the paper was published and I have given several talks on the subject. So keeping an open mind even while having a difficult period in your life or career can lead to an unexpected event and something beneficial.

So the advice I can give is to always look to find ways to help others or find things or ideas that are beneficial to you, whether or not you have had a problem in your career or personal life. By keeping your eyes and mind open and always being ready, you may be able to achieve things out of a routine or troublesome time. Stay ready with your eyes and mind open in the usual activities of your life or while working toward a goal as Chris Hadfield did. In that way you can also enjoy the ride rather than always looking toward the destination. And be ready for that unexpected event even when you are in the midst of adversity or troubling times. In doing so, you are likely to come across multiple serendipitous opportunities that you can use to your advantage and for the betterment of others.

CHAPTER 5
CURIOSITY DOESN'T
ALWAYS KILL THE CAT

W hen most people hear the word *curiosity*, they usually think of someone being nosy or constantly moving from one thing to another. This type of curiosity is best seen in toddlers, who are constantly on the move and exploring their world. However, this type of curiosity in adults is often distracting and frustrating. Engaging in it never allows you to get the full information you desire, and it feels unfulfilling. A deeper, more thoughtful type of curiosity is what often is necessary if one is to become successful with a serendipitous event. In his book *Curious*, Ian Leslie, a London journalist and author of many books on psychology and behavior, terms this type of curiosity *epistemic*, and it deserves some exploration as to what its origins are and how it plays a major role in utilizing serendipitous events to their fullest. In this chapter we explore epistemic curiosity, as well as another type of curiosity termed *empathic curiosity*, which deals with curiosity about other individuals: their life stories, interests, and feelings. This is essential for physicians and others who have close relationships with those they serve.

Where Curiosity Arises

Epistemic curiosity is a search for a deeper understanding of something that we have encountered. It may be the exploration of a novel or non-fiction book, or an experiment designed by a scientist. The driving force of epistemic curiosity is the lack of a complete understanding of the topic. The quest for knowledge of a particular subject characterizes epistemic curiosity, as opposed to the superficial recognition that occurs with regular curiosity. When we encounter a gap in a particular knowledge, we are driven to find out what we can on the subject. This type of curiosity begins in childhood when the child is seeking some independence from his or her parents. It seems paradoxical, but it has been shown that the more people know about a particular area, the more they become curious about the information that they don't have. Epistemic curiosity actually breeds more curiosity about that subject and others related to it. Conversely, with regular curiosity, a small amount of knowledge on the subject satisfies one's curiosity.

But how does this relate to serendipity? The answer lies in the nature of a serendipitous event and how one approaches that event. As I have indicated, observational skills are a key component of recognizing something useful in the field one is working in. Once the observation is recognized, the next step involves curiosity. You may recognize that a tree you have come upon in the forest is different from all the other trees. Some people may shrug their shoulders, say to themselves, "That's odd," and walk on. But "interesting" patients. She wanted to teach them the mantra we all had as academic general internists, that there are *no* uninteresting patients. She challenged her residents to pick the least interesting patient on their service, so she could show them something interesting about her. They chose an elderly woman who was admitted simply because she had been evicted and could not care for herself, so she was awaiting placement. When questioned, the woman simply said she had been a hotel maid, had an uninteresting life, and had no medical illnesses. As Faith was getting desperate, she finally asked her if she had been born in San Francisco, to which the patient replied that she had come from Ireland in 1912. Faith went on to inquire as to whether the patient had ever been in a hospital. She indicated that she had, once, for a broken arm. When asked how it occurred, she indicated that a trunk had fallen on it. Faith was perplexed and asked what kind of trunk, to which the woman replied that it was a steamer trunk. Faith went on to ask how this had happened, and the woman indicated that the boat she was on had lurched. When asked why it had lurched, she replied that the boat had hit the ice. What was the name of the boat? The *Titanic*. The woman was suddenly the center of attention to the house staff and the local media.

I have not had someone who was on the *Titanic* as a patient, or anything nearly as significant, but I have had some very interesting people in my practice since coming to San Diego. Their stories would never have been uncovered had I not been curious and asked questions about them. The first one was an elderly gentleman whom I saw when I first arrived. He came to me for a routine first visit in which we went over his health history and treatment. He had a very strong French accent, and when I asked him what he did, he said he was retired. I then asked him what he used to do, and he said he was an oceanographer at the Scripps Oceanographic Institute. I went on to ask other questions and was still curious about how he arrived in San Diego, so I asked him where he had trained. He told me he had gotten his degree at the Sorbonne. I couldn't restrain myself, and looking at him directly, asked, "Did you know him?" He didn't need to be told I was asking about Jacques Cousteau, the most well-recognized oceanographer and inventor of the Aqua-Lung, the earliest successful scuba tank. My patient smiled broadly, and said that Jacques Cousteau had been his main mentor, had taught him to sail and scuba dive, and gave him his first set of sails for his own sailboat.

Another retired patient came in to see me for the first time several years later. When asked what he had done before retirement, he indicated that he was an engineer. "What type of engineering?" I asked. He replied that he had been trained and worked actively in aeronautical engineering. At this point in this book it is likely clear that I have always had a side passion for the aeronautical field, unless it is an area within that field that is completely over my head (for example, I don't know a lot about different types of aircraft engines). Even then, however, I may still find some interest in the prospect of learning something new. In this case, I asked him what company he worked for, and he said he worked for Grumman. I have some knowledge of World War II history, and so I knew that Grumman designed and built the Navy fighters used in the Pacific Theater (F4F Wildcat and F6F Hellcat), but he was too young to have been involved in those designs and production. I knew Grumman later made some jet fighters and something else that I just wasn't able to think of at that visit. So patient at the VA had complained of a similar instance, stating that it was common for patients to receive information of a communicable disease in a non-private manner while on active duty. That patient was upset since he was embarrassed when other soldiers heard the information and saw his response to getting the information.

It dawned on me that perhaps this was a common occurrence in the armed services; if so, it needed to be brought to light and it needed to change. Although this was before the HIPPA legislation was passed, there had always been an ethical tenet that patients had a right to privacy. I made the connection that if two patients in separate settings, but both in the active military, were informed of their HIV status in a clearly non-private and unethical manner, other patients in a similar setting or in the Veterans Affairs medical system might have the same experiences. We designed a questionnaire that asked patients who had informed them of their HIV diagnosis, how much time was spent counseling the patient on safe sex practices (to protect sexual partners) and counseling about AIDS, and the perceived emotional and educational support given.

Out of 140 patients at the Philadelphia VA who were diagnosed (at that time) with HIV infection, 102 agreed to complete the questionnaire. Eighteen of the patients were informed of the diagnosis in non-private settings, such as in a waiting room, by mail, and even, in one case, with a message left on an answering machine. Respondents were evenly split on the amount of education delivered about safe sex and AIDS (52.6% indicated someone talked a lot or somewhat about it, while 47.4% indicated either it was talked about only a little or not at all). The amount of perceived emotional support was better but not ideal: 61.2% felt they received a lot or some emotional support, while 38.8% felt they received little or no emotional support. The report was published in the *Journal of General Internal Medicine* and led to changes in how sensitive information like HIV infection was delivered to patients.

Many of the serendipitous experiences in science and industry that I have described occurred after the observation and curiosity of the individual was extended to include connections with previous information that was available. For example, when Edison pricked his finger with the vibrating needle attached to the diaphragm of the telephone he was experimenting with, he was curious about whether the vibrations from the needle would etch lines in soft material that could then be used to recreate the sound. He made the connection that as a needle on a telephone diaphragm vibrated, it might be able to permanently recreate that sound in some fashion on another device.

Making connections can often be an essential part of projects or missions which otherwise might never have successfully occurred. Such was the case with the first manned lunar landing. NASA always did simulations of its missions ever since the Mercury missions (the first U.S. manned space flights). These simulations were not only for the astronauts who would fly the missions; they also provided training for the engineers in Mission Control. Before the Apollo 11 mission in July 1969, Richard Koos, the simulation supervisor, was running a simulation for the backup crew of Apollo 12, but mainly for the folks in Mission Control. He decided to throw them a curve ball: He simulated a computer alarm in the lunar module (LM), something the engineers had not previously experienced. The alarm, coded 1201, was due to the computer having to deal with too much landing radar data at once. It was a benign alarm as long as the computer continued to be operational and no other problems (such as a fault in the landing radar) were determined. However, NASA had no written rules regarding computer alarms.

So when the alarm occurred during the simulation, Steve Bales, the computer expert, informed Gene Kranz, the team head in Mission Control (known as Flight), that it was an "executive overflow," meaning the computer was overloaded with data. When Kranz turned to Jack Garman, his software expert, he was made aware that the computer was overly busy, but what the consequences would be were unknown. Kranz then made the decision to abort the mission during the simulation. At the debrief, he was informed by Richard Koos in no uncertain terms that he had erred by calling the abort instead of continuing the landing. Koos said that it was just the computer operating on a priority scheme and dealing with a lot of data, but if the guidance, radar, thrusters, and engine were all working and the displays were all as they should be, the landing was safe to go on.

Two weeks later, as Neil Armstrong and Buzz Aldrin in the *Eagle* were in the descent toward the lunar landing, they got a warning light in the cockpit with a 1202 computer alarm. Jack Garman reported the alarm to Steve Bales, who told Flight to stand by. Charlie Duke, the capsule communicator (or capcom, a term left over from when the Mercury missions consisted of a capsule instead of a command module), who had been in the simulation two weeks before, remembered that they had experienced a similar alarm at that time. Gene Kranz, upon hearing that, instantly made the connection: these alarms were benign as long as everything else was working. He therefore told Charlie Duke as capcom to inform Armstrong and Aldrin they were still go for the landing and that they could ignore the alarm (though each alarm did have to be reviewed to be sure no serious problems existed with the computer). Due to the simulation and connections made during it, the landing went ahead and made history instead of being aborted.

A more explicit example that I described in the first chapter was the way in which the smallpox vaccine was discovered. When Edward Jenner, a physician in late eighteenth century England, overheard the dairymaid talk about how she could never get potentially fatal smallpox since she had already gotten cowpox, a lesser, only annoying disease that dairymaids often contracted from cows, he needed to make connections to come up with the smallpox vaccine. The belief that contracting cowpox had prevented milkmaids from getting smallpox was simply folklore at that time, but over the years Jenner recognized that there might be some truth to the tale. Jenner made the connection between the milkmaids' tale and the observation that they had a lack of infection with smallpox. He began to think that there might be something in the pox of the cowpox disease that somehow would protect people from smallpox.

Many years later, Jenner collected material from cowpox lesions and inoculated the arm of a young boy, whom he exposed to smallpox eight weeks later. The boy did not get smallpox, and thereafter Jenner experimented more avidly with cowpox inoculation. It soon became apparent that Jenner had discovered a preventative agent for smallpox, which then became mandatory throughout the world. Because Jenner was able to make the connections that some agent in the cowpox inoculation (he didn't know anything about the immune system at that time) prevented an individual from getting smallpox when later exposed, he developed the vaccine that would eventually eradicate smallpox from the world by December 1979.

Sometimes one might even make connections after a dream. In my case you are reading the results of that dream as I described earlier. Such an occurrence allowed David Parkinson to discover the gun director, which helped improve the accuracy of Allied anti-aircraft guns during World War II. The gun director was a mechanical computer device that aimed the guns that were directed against enemy airplanes. In the spring of 1940, Germany was on the move, and the Allies were in trouble, especially from the German Luftwaffe. Parkinson had a dream one night in which he was with the Dutch as they were firing their guns into the sky to try to bring down the German planes. The Dutch soldiers fired multiple shells from their guns. In actual practice, the Allies had to fire thousands of shells to bring down one plane. In his dream, Parkinson noted that with each shot fired by the Dutch soldiers, another German plane crashed to the ground in flames, having been destroyed by the anti-aircraft shell. Parkinson was amazed at the unusual accuracy of the Dutch guns, and when he looked closer, he noticed a small, round mechanism mounted on top of the gun.

Parkinson awoke and recalled the dream. He recognized the round object: it was a potentiometer, a device that controlled movement and which Parkinson used as an engineer in a machine called a strip recorder, which made marks on paper (the classic example being the strip of paper recording an earthquake). He connected the dots: He thought that the potentiometer might be able to be used in some fashion to control the movements of anti-aircraft guns. He went on to develop the gun director, which adjusted the aim of anti-aircraft guns by constantly recalculating the position of the target airplane, as opposed to the relocation of guns previously by just estimating the plane's location, speed, and direction. The number of shells fired to bring down one airplane went from thousands to less than one hundred. It was the gun director that helped stem the tide of the German Luftwaffe onslaught.

It is clear that most scientific and technical research requires some kind of connection in order to be successful. Once you have the mindset that unexpected events can occur, and have recognized one due to your observational skills and explored it due to your curiosity about the event or idea, it is the connections you make between the event and your previous experiences and knowledge that bring the unexpected event into the light. The connections allow the "aha" moment to occur. Putting all of it together then happens, and I will share some examples next.

PART III

Go:
Making It Happen

Going from the occurrence of a serendipitous event to the productive outcome as a result of that event usually requires a great deal of effort on your part. You must first acquire the four skills (an open mind, observational skills, curiosity, and being able to make connections) in order to recognize the serendipitous event and determine if it is worthwhile to pursue it. The combination of self-awareness and having an open mind is the necessary foundation. This allows you to be on the lookout for unexpected events. Observational skills (whether seeing or hearing something unexpected) allow for the triggering event to be consciously recognized. Rachel wouldn't have noticed the slight edge of the penny sticking out from under the leaf if she didn't have keen observational skills. Curiosity is usually required to lead you to explore what is occurring. And sometimes you need to be able to connect the unexpected event with previously learned information or previous experiences, as Sir Alexander Fleming did when he realized that something was being secreted by the mold into the culture medium. Once you have these skills and recognize the fortuitous event as such, it often requires more advanced particular skills (perhaps equipment and space) and support in other ways, in addition to effort on your part. I will discuss all of this in this third part of the book.

Once you actually have recognized the event and have worked on it enough to have a specific outcome or product, you may then need to promote it or have someone else do so. But this is not the final chapter in an unexpected event's history. Even when your idea or product has taken off and you and/or society are profiting from it, people can have declining interest, or the idea or product may even backfire. The occurrences may still generate profitable outcomes from unexpected events, even though they may not be all that one expected. It is important to understand how to carefully analyze each unexpected event in order to assess its worth to you and to society in order to avoid these circumstances, or how to cope with them if they are unavoidable. So this section covers how to gain the know-how to recognize serendipity, make it into a profitable (monetary or otherwise) idea or product, and how to maintain resilience if it ends up being somewhat less than you had hoped for.

CHAPTER 8
GETTING THE SKILLS

One of my main mentors, Frank Davidoff, told me the story of a young but fantastic violinist about to make his debut with the New York Philharmonic one evening. On his way to the concert, he got off the subway at the wrong station and was beside himself at his mistake. He walked over to an older gentleman sitting on a bench on Seventh Avenue and asked him how he could get to Carnegie Hall. The gentleman took in the young man carrying a violin case and offered the advice, "Practice, practice, practice."

Practice is the only way to acquire the skills necessary for the recognition of serendipity. You may have been practicing and using these skills all along as I have. Many of us practice and use these skills unconsciously because of the type of work they do. My own interests and the way that I think (perhaps *had* to think in order to become a clinician-educator-scientist in general internal medicine) prepared me to recognize serendipity while it was happening or shortly after its occurrence. However, if you don't innately have these skills, or you don't operate in a type of work that requires them on a daily basis, you may need to consciously and frequently practice them. I will provide you with some tips and examples of where each of these skills can be practiced.

Practice Being Aware

The foundation of developing an open mind is the practicing of self-awareness. We teach these skills to our first-year medical students in one of the classes that I lead. We use a combination of exercises, one of which involves closing your eyes, putting a raisin in your mouth, and without chewing, thinking about what you are experiencing. We also have them do exercises in meditation. There are many exercises in self-awareness available online. For example, one exercise that I saw online (The Check-In Exercise, Dr. Jennifer Franklin") asks you to ask questions about yourself. Ask yourself about your past, present, and future. This is a good way to understand how you react to things and why. There are also several books available on developing self-awareness, such as *Mindfulness for Beginners: Reclaiming the Present Moment of Your Life by Jon Kabat-Zinn*; and "*The Little Book of Being: Practice and Guidance for Uncovering Your Natural Awareness by Diana Winston*.

There are lots of applications on your smartphone or in various books that will allow you to practice both visual and auditory observational skills. If you like using your phone to occasionally play games, you can make your playtime substantially more valuable by downloading and using these apps. Some of the best apps for visual skills are ones where you need to determine how one photo or drawing is different from another since it has been purposely changed. The challenge is to find all of the things that have been changed. I went into the app store for my iPhone and found fifty games that I could download (most for free) by putting in the search term "photo difference games." These are great for training your eyes and brain to notice subtle differences. Other games that can help are mystery games where you need to spot clues in the "murder scene." Some are fashioned like an escape room (you have to find clues in order to escape from the room you are "locked up in"), while in others you are a detective trying to solve the murder. If you don't have a smartphone, a lot of these games are available for your computer, and some even in paper form (I found dozens of both types on Amazon).

Focusing on one aspect of what is around you can cause you to overlook some of the more interesting details. Search on You-Tube for "Take the Awareness Test." Spoiler alert! (Don't read the next sentences if you want to be surprised.) In the video, there are four guys in white clothing and four in black who are passing a basketball around. The instructions are to count the number of times someone in white passes the ball to someone else. You focus on counting the number of times as the video plays, and you determine that it was passed thirteen times. The narrator then asks if you saw the moonwalking bear (what?!). The video is then replayed, and while you are not focusing on specifically how many times the ball is passed by those in white, you clearly see that in the middle of the video someone dressed in a black bear suit walks into the middle of the game and starts moonwalking. That is what focusing on too specific a task and not having enough self-awareness and keen observational skills can do.

Auditory skills can also be honed by games in which the listener needs to pick out sounds or words that are different between two verbal renditions of a story. These are also available in apps for your smartphone, computer, or in paper form, but they are less available than visual games. You can also buy board games that enhance verbal skills. Games like Bad Actor (a character impersonation game) and Outburst can enhance listening skills. Is it silly to be playing games when I am talking about trying to obtain skills necessary for recognizing serendipity? Not if they work for you. These are just some tips. Whatever you find helpful in this vein is an advantage. Briefly look at the image below and then keep reading at the top of the next page.

insights and was able to do so by making connections, i.e., seeing ways in which ideas, thoughts, and observations interact and how they may be developed into something greater.

I am experienced in making connections because of my training as a physician, but if you are not experienced, you can learn to do so in many ways. To start, there are several books on how to think in a way that allows for problem solving. Two of the books I have come across are *Thinking Fast and Slow* by Daniel Kaneman, a psychologist and winner of the Nobel Prize in Economics and the 2011 Presidential Medal of Freedom, and *The Art of Thinking Clearly* by Rolf Dobelli. Books and articles about how physicians process information, such as *How Doctors Think* by Jerome Groopman, can be of benefit. The key is to reflect on what unexpected event or experience has occurred. Then think about any other experiences or information you have read that was similar in some way to the current event. Once you make that connection, you can begin to more thoroughly explore the event, connecting the experience and prior experiences or knowledge.

Regular mystery books are also a good source for practicing making connections, but puzzles are not a good way to practice this skill. As Ian Leslie states, puzzles have definite answers, whereas mysteries pose questions that must be addressed. We don't encounter an unexpected event with an answer in mind, nor do we usually find one answer during our exploration of the event. There may be multiple ways of addressing the things that we encounter, and we have to think creatively and logically to be successful in parsing through our options forward. Mystery-solving offers much better opportunities to practice these skills than a straightforward puzzle.

Reading as much as you can will also help with making connections in addition to enhancing your curiosity. Once you find something that you *are* curious about, you can start reading some literature or reading online in that area. It is a good idea to start writing down aspects of what you have read and, most importantly, thoughts that come to you as you read. You will find that you suddenly are asking questions and developing ideas that relate to each other. As this occurs, you will begin making connections. This can lead to an exploration of those events you have encountered in the past, and can lay the groundwork for recognizing the serendipitous event or ideas that you will encounter in the future. There are also a lot of programs available online for teaching kids how to make connections with their ideas, but many are also targeted at adults. Any of these programs can be useful; try a few and see which work for you. The most important thing is to keep active in reading and thinking along these lines. Remember that no idea, resource, or experience is inappropriate when you are investigating it. One idea or observation may not be fruitful, but eventually you will find something worthwhile.

Opening Your Mind

Let's go back to the photo I showed you several pages ago. Even if I had printed it in color, and you noticed the rainbow, how would you respond if I asked you to place yourself in the car and tell me what you were feeling? Perhaps most people would say, "Oh wow! Look at that rainbow." But I suspect a fair number would say, "Yuck. It's raining." The latter might be less likely to decide to *do* something with a serendipitous event, even if it might allow for some improvement in one's life or in society as a whole. Though no research has been conducted on this, some psychologists have theorized that people with a pessimistic attitude toward unexpected and serendipitous events are less likely to take advantage of such events. So everyone who encounters a serendipitous event and wants to enhance their career or life needs to have an open mind to explore what the event holds for them. If you start with a negative attitude, it is unlikely that you will recognize the serendipitous event when it occurs. There is a lot of information online and in books about practicing how to keep an open mind, as I discussed previously in this chapter.

Keeping an open mind involves going outside of your comfort zone. This is an essential aspect of recognizing serendipity and taking advantage of it. As Ian Leslie states, success and complacency, that is, a reluctance to go outside one's comfort zone, are really counterproductive when it comes to curiosity. If you are successful and therefore complacent, you tend to resist going outside your comfort zone instead of seeking new ideas. Leaders of corporations can also become trapped in success and complacency; they look inward instead of being interested in other ideas. Leaders who are interested in what they don't know as opposed to what they already have are more successful in the business world. It's risky to be outside of your comfort zone, but it is necessary and will become exciting when you encounter something you hadn't thought of previously.

The first and easiest way of challenging yourself is to try something new. Obviously, the list of possibilities is endless, and it really depends on what *you* might find challenging and beyond your comfort zone. You might try reading a type of literature you usually don't read about a subject you aren't familiar with or in which you are not usually interested. For example, if you usually read non-fiction books about a certain topic (for me it's space and aircraft), you might try reading a romance novel. Or you might try poetry. Anything that is outside your usual frame of reference is useful. Or you might try listening to a different type of music, one you usually don't like. Listen to the rhythm, the meaning it conveys to you.

You could also try other new things, such as types of food that you have never eaten before. What are the tastes like? What was the entire experience at the restaurant like? Some authors suggest other new things, like taking a class in something you never experienced before (this does involve a time commitment). Others suggest traveling to new places. Since retiring, I have started to explore the national parks in the western states. I had never gone to a national park before coming to San Diego fourteen years ago. I had never traveled alone, always going places with Terry. We did go to Grand Canyon National Park during one trip, and to Yosemite and Joshua Tree National Parks during others. But we were always together. Terry can't really travel any longer, so I set out for one national park (Zion) on my own. I was scared, as I was hiking the trails by myself. What if I should fall or get hurt? Of course, nothing happened, and it was fantastic to be on the trails, totally out of my comfort zone, as I was by myself. I really learned a lot about myself during that trip and others. Not only do I now go to other national parks by myself, I have taken up hiking as a hobby. And my experiences have led to thinking a lot about the various skills I use when encountering unexpected events.

You can really challenge yourself with new experiences and by meeting new people. You might try attending a service of a

CHAPTER 9
ROLL UP YOUR SLEEVES

In taking advantage of a serendipitous event, you are being an innovator. You are recognizing its occurrence and deciding to pursue it so that a suitable idea or product can be brought to society, with the added benefit of reward to you in the realm of career enhancement, fame, and/or monetary gain. Great, right? But the first thing to realize is that innovation involves two things: exploration and exploitation. Exploration involves recognizing and investigating the serendipitous event. That is what Einstein did when he developed the Theory of Relativity from his initial musings on the idea. Einstein kept an open mind. He was curious. He utilized all of the skills we learned in previous chapters are essential to recognizing unexpected events.

Exploitation involves continuation of the effort begun with recognizing the unexpected event. It is what all great innovators did *after* they recognized the serendipitous event. Henry Ford did not discover the automobile nor the assembly line; he merely worked on both ideas to the extent that he was immensely successful in producing an automobile in a short period of time, and one that the average American could afford.

Exploitation, or the refining of something that is already present and known, is an important part of serendipity. Thomas Edison is famous for his exploitation in the "development" of the light bulb. The light bulb had been developed years earlier, but they were short-lived due to the burning out of the filament. Edison made a more practical light bulb by using tungsten in a vacuum-filled glass bulb so that the filament lasted much longer and produced better lighting. Exploitation is also important when other unexpected events occur after the basic research has been completed.

Of the forty serendipitous events I referenced, ten did not mention how long it took to bring the discovery to fruition. Only six had immediate results, and interestingly, they all involved archeologic or pure scientific finds (the Dead Sea Scrolls; the uncovering of Pompeii; the discovery of the Lascaux cave drawings; the discovery of ancient human bones; the development of the structure of benzene; and the discovery of the relationship of weight, volume, and density discovered by Archimedes). One of the remaining twenty-four discoveries was an outlier, taking fifty-nine years to fully develop the smallpox vaccine. If we still include it in the calculation, the amount of time it took on average to bring these ideas and products to success was 10.2 years. However, even without that one as an outlier, the remaining twenty-three discoveries required on average 8.17 years to fully develop. So the first thing you need to decide is whether it is worthwhile to pursue the serendipitous event you have come across. It requires some thought and estimation of what will be required, the amount of time needed, and what the outcome will be.

Is It Worth It?

Often it is worth the investment to bring an event to full success. Most of my research endeavors cost little in time and money, and I felt it was worth the effort. However, some research that takes more time, effort, and money can still very much be worth the costs. Such an event was the discovery of the nicotine patch.

In 1981, Frank Etscorn worked in a basement laboratory in the New Mexico Institute of Mining and Technology, experimenting with sugar dependency in laboratory rats. He was using liquid nicotine from tobacco plants to see if the nausea it produced could decrease the rats' craving for sugar. One day he tripped while carrying a beaker of the substance and splashed some accidentally on his arm. It was highly concentrated; he wiped it off but did not wash the arm. After fifteen minutes he suddenly became nauseated himself. He made some connections, realizing that putting nicotine on the skin would be a convenient way of getting it into the bloodstream, and then that it might help people to quit smoking. Etscorn started experimenting on himself and his brother John, swabbing different concentrations of nicotine on the skin and later developing a patch that would release the nicotine into the skin over time. By 1986, five years later, Etscorn had a reliable patch that he patented and thereafter sold, bringing the nicotine patch to market and reaping monetary rewards for himself. I would imagine he felt that the five years' worth of work was worth it.

Conversely, sometimes such an endeavor is not worth the financial and time costs involved. We previously discussed Charles Goodyear's attempt to bring vulcanization to fruition. It took many years of experimentation, large sums of money, and much frustration until he finally patented a reasonable process. However, after selling the patent (and gaining fame for it), he was penniless and reaped no real monetary rewards. So how do you decide?

Much of the decision lies with what skills and resources are available to you. It is not surprising that most of the innovators I have cited in this book had the skills necessary to experiment with the discovery, many of whom worked for a company that provided them with the laboratories, assistants, and tools they needed. The first time I decided to do a study on my own in 1982, I took only a slight risk. I had been taught about survey research, and used only a small group of residents as my subjects at Hahnemann University in Philadelphia. I did have both clinical and teaching responsibilities, but was able to mange the time needed to develop the questionnaire, administer it, do the analysis, and complete the paper for submission. Even so, it did take a many months.

Later on in my career (for example, the capital punishment surveys), the research was much more complex. I needed to perform an extensive literature search to ensure the study I was considering had not been previously done and to obtain background information, develop the questionnaire, test it among a sample of subjects to ensure the questions I was asking were correctly interpreted and understood by the subjects, obtain Institutional Review Board approval, mail out the surveys twice (we did not have online surveys like we do now; I had to print and fold surveys and stuff and stamp envelopes), enter data in a statistics program and do the analysis, and write up the paper. The total time it took was about two years for each study. But it was worth it to find out the answers to my questions and be recognized for the work I was doing. In fact, much of the scientific research mentioned in this book only took a few years at most to come to a suitable point where the innovator could reap the benefits. But only you can decide whether the event you have stumbled across is worth the time and resources that you will be investing.

One more note of caution here. Gail Sheehy, in her famous book *Passages*, talks about the fact that when we go from one phase of our lives to another, for example leaving our parents to make our own way in the world, it is the internal factors (our own feelings, psychological issues, et cetera) that cause us to make the transition, not those that are external to us, such as job opportunities. Sure, the transition often involves a change, but that change stems from the psychological issues that we have. However, often someone happens upon a serendipitous event and believes that it is the solution to their troubles. Nothing could be further from the truth. Yes, it may *fit in* with everything that is occurring, but it is not likely to be an answer. You need to examine the idea, product, or event for its own value, weighing that against the time and resources needed rather than factoring in how it may benefit your career or life. You need to do the work for its own sake, not for the potential payouts. Of course, if the event is one that involves a job or career change, it is different, and does require an analysis of how it will affect you.

Get What You Need

Unless you are independently wealthy with advanced degrees in whatever area of focus you are pursuing, it is likely you will need to get some resources and perhaps assistance for what you will be doing. This can help you decide what to do with what you have found. Here are some tips on getting the resources and assistance you need to be able to continue the research you are conducting on the unexpected event or trying to decide about whether to engage in such research.

Find Someone More Experienced Than You

If you look at most of the discoveries that have occurred in a serendipitous manner, the people who were able to perform research about the event and take advantage of the discovery were all researchers in those fields. For example, Sir Alexander Fleming was both a physician and microbiologist, doing research in the field of microbiology when he stumbled across the mold that yielded penicillin. It is not surprising that those in the field are often the ones who bring the serendipitous event to light and to fulfillment, since they have the expertise and experience needed to know how to conduct the necessary research after the event is discovered. But what if you stumble across an event that is not in your field? The key is to seek assistance. Yes, the expert whom you contact will likely share in the rewards for the discovery, but it is necessary if you want to gain the fame and/or monetary rewards that may be forthcoming.

One way to make a connection is to seek out a mentor who can help you strategize. Mentors are individuals who are older and more experienced in the field you are trying to break into. Frank Davioff was one of my main mentors at the University of Connecticut in my first attending position after residency. Through Davidoff, I was introduced to other amazing mentors in my own field and outside it. Without these mentors, my horizons would have been noticeably less broad. This was the start of my research career. You can usually find mentors at either universities, in industry, or in societies devoted to the area in which you are interested.

Another way of getting assistance is by directly recruiting someone to help you who is experienced in the field. After several projects that I conducted on my own after learning what I needed about survey research, I found myself being recruited as an experienced researcher in that technique. I was suddenly sought out by others in each of the institutions where I was working who were interested in using a survey technique to analyze values or self-reports of physicians, students, residents, or patients. Of the approximately sixty papers that I have published, fifteen involved an area distant from my interests and expertise except that they involved survey research. In those fifteen, another individual asked me to assist in conducting a survey. These individuals included psychiatrists, a student interested in physiatry (physical medicine and rehabilitation), and other general internal medicine physicians in my division who were interested in topics other than the ones (medical ethics and patient-physician relationship) I have always studied. I was asked to be involved since those individuals had no experience conducting surveys, and they wanted to do so. Even if you have expertise in the field, you may still need to contact someone to assist you in a specific aspect of your research. For example, many physicians in our medical school contact those in the engineering school to help with ideas they have involving the development of an instrument or device involved in diagnosing or treating medical illnesses.

Getting Resources

If you don't already work for a company or university with labs you have access to, you may need space (office, laboratory, et cetera) and resources (equipment, chemicals, or other lab equipment depending on what the discovery is) to further research your area. I was fortunate in that my interests lay in the realm of social psychology, so that my only needs (besides time) were access to a computer and statistical package and, at times, small amounts of cash for buying lists of physicians (the AMA maintains such lists), paper for the surveys, and postage (along with, at times, a monetary incentive). I was able to have all this thanks to the institutions where I worked, as they were often interested in promoting my work. But if you need more complex and expensive resources, you may need to seek out funding for the research. Mentors can also help you in this regard, but if there is commercial gain possible on the basis of the discovery, you may be able to negotiate a deal with a company. Someone who is on the inside of the firm can often help. You can search for those with similar interests by going to various firms' websites or by asking someone in the local university if they have contacts with manufacturing firms, as they often do.

For example, in San Diego there are a large number of aerospace and other engineering firms that the Department of Engineering has contact with. We saw that the discovery of whipped cream in a can was such an event where the assistance of a manufacturing firm was crucial in its eventual success. This research was spearheaded by a student working for a professor who, it so happened, had established a small company apart from the university. It is often the case that faculty have contacts with manufacturing firms, although sometimes even a separate firm may be interested in what you have discovered (think *Shark Tank*, the TV program in which investors offer to get involved in a start-up business often based on a serendipitous discovery). You can also seek loans or grants. As an example, one firm in San Diego called Founders First Capital Partners helps small businesses run by minorities or veterans to secure loans and grants for capital investments.

Another option is to sell your discovery to a company with the resources to investigate it further. The caution here, though, is to be careful how this is done. I am *not* an expert in this area, and you may need to seek legal counsel. Some have sold their discovery for a small amount with no percentage of the profits promised in writing, then looked on without financial reward while the company made a huge profit on a successful product.

The final step, and one you may need help with, is manufacturing the product or presenting to the world your idea or product once it is fully developed. Do you have the resources to do this, or will you need help? Most people do not have the resources unless it is a small contribution, such as a research paper like the ones I have published. Most journals in the past published such articles for free once they were accepted; some still do, but more are now charging fees into the thousands of dollars, citing the fact that they no longer accept advertising. This is still reasonable for someone who has other sources of income.

However, sometimes the cost of manufacturing and publicizing a product or idea can be enormous, and you may need help with the costs and resources. In these cases, selling your idea or product is the best way of accomplishing this. However, the goal is to get the idea or product well enough publicized first, so that you are sought after by many large corporations. For example, Ben

& Jerry's Ice Cream was founded by Ben Cohen (who dropped out of college) and Jerry Greenfield (who graduated college but was unable to get into medical school as he wished) in 1978 with a $12,000 loan when they opened an ice cream parlor in Burlington, Vermont, after taking an ice-cream-making course at Pennsylvania State University. They had been friends since childhood and made a terrific pair: Cohen had anosmia (lack of smell), so relied on the texture of the ice cream, while Greenfield had a good sense of taste and smell. When they started putting textured foods like chocolate chunks into their ice cream because of Cohen's anosmia, and had patrons in their small ice cream parlor go wild over it, they knew they had a hit (their "aha" moment). They were wildly popular, and in 1980 began packaging the ice cream in pints from rented space in an old factory in Burlington, then started to franchise Ben & Jerry's ice cream parlors in other parts of New England, eventually shipping their ice cream around the country. So who *wouldn't* want a piece of this action? In 2000, Ben & Jerry's was sold to the British-Dutch conglomerate Unilever for $326 million. Not everyone can do this, but if you can take out a small loan and work up a successful idea or product, you too may be able to sell it for quite a profit.

Another option is to work up the product or idea and negotiate with a company to have them take over the production for a share of the profits. This requires some knowledge of the various companies that might be interested and whether they have acted on behalf of small companies in the past in a similar fashion. You may want to protect yourself in these situations by having a corporate attorney on your side. Ben & Jerry's did have to fight against Pillsbury Company several times in 1984, 1985, and 1987 when the company tried to limit distribution of Ben & Jerry's in Boston. Each time Pillsbury, which had bought Häagen-Dasz Ice Cream, threatened to stop allowing distributors to sell their product if they also sold Ben & Jerry's. Häagen-Dasz was the distributors' major product, and they could not afford to lose it.

In 1984, when Cohen and Greenfield contacted their attorney, they were told that they could file a restraint of trade lawsuit, but that they wouldn't get anywhere since Pillsbury was a $4 billion corporation. So Cohen and Greenfield started a campaign with the slogan, "What's the doughboy afraid of?" They had customers mass calling and writing Pillsbury about their unfair practices, and Pillsbury eventually relented. However, a year later, when Pillsbury went back to the tactics of threatening its distributors, Ben & Jerry's did file suit and won an injunction against Pillsbury, which had to be repeated in 1987. Since then, Häagen-Dasz and Ben & Jerry's have peacefully coexisted.

Sometimes there may be others interested in your idea or product, depending on its nature. Often, a non-profit foundation may give money for some things, such as the Give a Soap Foundation, which donates leftover soaps from hotels to homeless shelters in New York and New Jersey. You can pitch your idea to such a foundation (if it fits) or start your own foundation. Many foundations will donate funds to help start other foundations. You won't make lots of cash from such an effort, but your idea will definitely get known. In addition, governments, including the U.S. government, may be interested in your idea or product if it has benefits for the state or country. The best sources for U.S. or other loans or grants are online. Check out the U.S. government website at GovLoans.gov for information on loans. There are also loans sponsored by the Small Business Association, opportunities for obtaining investment capital, and information on where to apply for grants at the website sba.gov. There are also a number of books on obtaining business loans and grants available through sites like Amazon. However, I am not sure of the authors' experience and therefore suggest you research them before purchasing their books.

Now that we have covered all of this, it is time to go out there and find your own serendipitous event! Well, not so fast. There are cautionary tales I must tell you about serendipitous events that backfired or fizzled out after a time, and why they did so. They still were serendipitous, often making quite a bit of fame and/or fortune for their inventors. But the key is knowing when to close down shop and how to do so.

CHAPTER 10
KNOW WHEN TO FOLD 'EM

S o you thought that once you encountered and developed an idea or product from a serendipitous event you were set for life, right? Well, sometimes yes, like Ben & Jerry, but sometimes no. When my father was in his twenties, he left South Fallsburg and moved to New York City. There he became an employee of the transit system. He met and married my mother there, and they had two children within four years of each other. Unfortunately, my oldest brother had a lot of allergies and mild asthma, and his physician advised my father that they should move back to the country to help his symptoms (actually the wrong move, since he was probably allergic to grasses and plants). They moved back to South Fallsburg, which had no transit system whatsoever. Needing to find a way of supporting his family and not wanting to enter the resort business, my father learned the plumbing trade. He eventually became so good at it and had such a good mind for estimating the cost of supplies and labor for plumbing jobs, that he set up his own business as a plumbing contractor.

In the 1950s and early 1960s, the Borscht Belt was booming, and my father's business was booming along with it. New hotels, shopping centers, and apartment and housing developments kept my father very busy and in a very good financial situation. But then things changed. The area was dependent on women staying at home with the family; they would come up for the summer with the kids to the bungalow colonies or hotels while the fathers worked in New York City and came up to the mountains on the weekends. But women started to enter the work force and could not come up to the resorts for the entire summer. The kids would go to summer camps, and the whole family had a two-week vacation for the entire summer. But why spend your two weeks going to the Catskills when Europe, California, and other places beckoned? The telltale sign of the societal change and consequent impending demise of the Catskills as a summer resort area was the dwindling occupancy of bungalow colonies and hotels. My father should have recognized those signs and made another move to a developing area such as the Sun Belt, which was booming, and where he could tolerate the weather given his heart condition. Instead he stayed and tried to weather the storm (or lack of it) and eventually went bankrupt. My father missed a golden opportunity by ignoring the signs of an unexpected event. Serendipity was therefore not his at this time.

Similar situations occur in the scientific and corporate worlds. Take, for instance, the Wham-O Company and the comparison between its sales of Frisbees and Hula-Hoops. Walter Frederick Morrison got the idea for a Frisbee when he and his wife, Lucille, had fun tossing a popcorn lid around in 1937. Someone on the beach approached them and offered twenty-five cents for their popcorn lid. Serendipitously, Morrison joined the U.S. Army Air Forces during World War II, where he flew a fighter and learned about aerodynamics. When he returned after the war, he developed the design for a plastic flying disc, which he named Pluto Platters, and with his partner, Warren Franscioni, began manufacture of the discs in 1948. Morrison was approached by the Wham-O Company and sold the rights in 1957. Wham-O renamed the flying disc "Frisbee," which sold well enough to now be a generic title for any plastic flying disc. Wham-O ended up selling more than 300 million Frisbees, and multiple times that number have been sold overall. There are now multiple flying disc sports (flying disc football, flying disc golf, et cetera), and the flying disc continues to be manufactured and sold by many different companies. Morrison ended up doing okay as well. His deal with Wham-O was for a royalty, and he ended up getting over $2 million in royalties over his lifetime.

On the other hand, Wham-O also marketed the Hula-Hoop. In 1957, Joan Anderson brought back a bamboo exercise hoop from Australia and renamed it the Hula-Hoop. Her husband showed it to Arthur Spiud Melin, a friend and businessman, and the two arranged its manufacture through Carlon Products Corporation, marketed by Wham-O. Unfortunately, since the Andersons did not patent the Hula-Hoop, Melin and Wham-O began the manufacture of Hula-Hoops independent of the Andersons. The Hula-Hoop fad began in 1958, and at that time Carlon Products Corporation was producing more than 50,000 Hula-Hoops per month. Within two years, sales reached 100 million. And then the bubble burst. The fad faded, and by the 1980s there were few Hula-Hoops sold except in Russia and China where the interest continued. But Wham-O did okay here as well; they ended up selling over 100 million Hula-Hoops before the fad died. The Andersons did not reap any benefits from its sales. As I stated in the last chapter, be sure you have legal advice before selling the rights of something you invented, discovered, or wrote about.

So why do some ideas and discoveries absolutely take off, and others fade into the "remember the..." realm? And if you are the discoverer of the latter, what should you do? This chapter will give you some ideas about how to try to avoid the bust, or what to do if you can't.

In my own experiences and in some of the literature I have reviewed, I can see three reasons why an idea, job, discovery, or otherwise serendipitous event ends up failing at some point. The first issue is that the person experiencing the event (yes, myself sometimes included) failed to properly analyze the discovery. It may be that the product or idea is faulty to begin with, proposed at the wrong time, or likely to fizzle quickly. In these cases you may yet get something out of it. The second reason that failures occur is because of some change in the culture (overall population, or in my case the corporate culture) which renders the idea, job, or product unsustainable. In these cases, it is most often a very valuable event that just cannot be sustained. But it still is valuable for the individual who recognizes and uses the unexpected event. The last is that there may be a change in *you* such that you no longer are interested in what you have encountered. In these cases, the event obviously is valuable in many different ways, but it may still be time to leave it behind. I shall give you examples from others as well as myself in all of these realms.

Failure From the Start

No one wants to hear that their idea will never work. But it is important to examine the idea yourself, have others review it, and come to that conclusion. I was very lucky in not having a serious failure occur. I believe I avoided these failures because of having wise mentors. However, I did periodically waste some time in pursuits that were not well examined. One of my early mentors was a brilliant physician and educator, Dr. Frank Sterling, who was the chief of endocrinology at the Philadelphia VA Medical Center in the 1970s and a professor of medicine at the University of Pennsylvania when I was a medical student there. Frank had done fantastic research and won multiple awards for his teaching. He could easily have gone on to be a division chief of endocrinology and ultimately a chairman of medicine and perhaps dean of the medical school at Penn or another highly ranked school. Why then did he choose not to do so? Frank was happy with the patient care, research, and especially the teaching that he was doing. Because of this, he was not interested in administration. As I considered these same issues throughout my own career, I realized I valued being a mentor of a group of physicians rather than being an administrative leader. The latter was not for me. I was offered those kinds of positions along the way and turned them down, as I would have been unhappy and not very good in those roles. Each time I thought about Frank and what I really wanted, I made decisions like Frank did.

Failure from the start does sometimes occur in the industrial world. Ever hear of R. Buckminster Fuller? He was a brilliant architect, engineer, and ecologist who firmly believed in meshing nature and technology to fulfill man's destiny on earth. He had a tremendous number of ideas, such that the magazine *Fortune* at one point paid him $15,000 per year (this is in the 1960s, with houses going at that price) just to come in and brainstorm for the editors. His most famous idea was the geodesic dome, which was a house in the shape of a dome built from individual triangles of structural material. He envisioned building domes that could cover whole cities up to a mile above the tallest buildings, yet be lighter than an ocean liner since the dome could be built as large as needed with light material and yet be structurally sound. Yet the geodesic dome never caught on. Because of the large number of joints, and with contraction in winter and expansion in summer, the dome proved very difficult to make watertight. Also, because of the fact that they were built of multiple triangles, and the dome-like structure itself, construction costs were much higher than for traditional buildings. Thus, actually manufacturing or building a geodesic dome was deemed to be more trouble than it was worth. Fuller, in his rush to accomplish his great ideas and ideals, forgot to consider the everyday factors that people must live with. However, he was widely recognized for this innovative idea, and certain specialty domes were created, the most notable today being Spaceship Earth at Epcot in Disney World.

The moral of this tale is that one must carefully and fully explore all angles when deciding whether to invest time, money, resources, and/or emotion in a potential outcome from a serendipitous event. Sometimes we find ourselves heady over the prospect of fame, enjoyment, and/or money and are blinded to the reality of the situation.

One minor example occurred in 1964. NASA was experimenting with ways of getting food to astronauts during the Mercury flights in the early 1960s. They developed the process of freeze-drying various foods and then reconstituting them with water. This allowed fresh fruits, vegetables and meats to be preserved and stored in lighter weight, smaller packages (a necessity in longer flights, as in the Gemini program and eventually Apollo flights to the moon). Post Company (manufacturer of cereals) thought adding freeze-dried fruit to a box of cereal, which would reconstitute when milk was added, would be a sure attraction for the average consumer of their products. So they added freeze-dried strawberries to boxes of their cornflakes. Sure enough, it was an instant hit, and in response they introduced freeze-dried peaches and blueberries, all manufactured in a new multimillion-dollar manufacturing facility. Kellogg's copied the idea with freeze-dried bananas added to its boxes of Corn Flakes.

So why was it that consumers would readily buy one box of the cereal, but no one was willing to buy a second box? Apparently, no one at Post or Kellogg's experimented enough with the product or waited long enough after adding milk to see how it held up. It took about ten minutes for the freeze-dried fruit to fully reconstitute when milk was added. However, the corn flakes sitting in the bowl with milk for ten minutes ended up turning to mush. No one who bought the product invested in a second box, and the idea came to a screeching halt. A little bit of further testing would have turned this up, but, understandably, Post was fired up with the initial tremendous success they had experienced. It is clearly important to do as much research on a product or idea as you can before deciding to go forward with it.

Another idea that came to fruition (sort of) was something called the Amphicar. The designer was a German engineer named Hans Trippel who had designed amphibious army vehicles for Germany in the 1950s. He decided to turn his talents toward a similar effort with an amphibious car for consumers. It was a convertible with the front wheels that served as rudders, and it had a 38-horsepower Triumph 4-cylinder engine. It wasn't bad on land, with a top speed of 72 miles per hour, but in the water it could only manage five miles per hour. About 2,500 Amphicars were produced in the 1960s, with many exported to the U.S. They thought that with the James Bond films going strong, such a car would appeal to many both in the U.S. and abroad.

However, only a modest number of the Amphicars were ever sold. Why, you might ask? There were a number of problems that were never thought of when the car was produced. First was the price tag: $3,395, which at that time would buy you a mid-range automobile along with a boat and trailer. Most people in either the United States or Germany, where the car originated, were not watercraft enthusiasts, or if they were, already owned a boat and trailer. In addition, although not especially fast on land, it was *very* slow in the water. Very few would buy something that would only function partly as a boat with that slow speed. Most people want a speed boat, unless they are interested in fishing (and even then, five miles per hour is used only when you are trawling for fish, not when you are getting out into the fishing grounds). At that speed, you can't pull a water skier or go very far. In addition, the car, made of automotive metal, tended to rust out after use in the water, especially when in sea water. This was not a complete flop for Trippel, as over 3,800 Amphicars were sold, including one to President Lyndon Johnson, who loved shocking unsuspecting visitors by driving into a lake on his ranch.

There have been more recent attempts at a faster amphibious automobile using a fiberglass body, jet pump propulsion, and retractable wheels, like the Aquastrada Delta in the 1990s. But at a price of $25,000 to $35,000, nothing much ever came of the attempt. It is always best to thoroughly test, including the population's attitudes and interest, before investing time, money, and resources in a project.

The scientific community may overlook some things about a possible discovery because they are so excited about the possibilities that they put aside some important basic scientific principles. Such an occurrence happened at the University of Pennsylvania in the late 1990s. There were gene therapy experiments at other institutions before those that took place at Penn; in 1990 the National Institutes of Health (NIH) engaged in the first human trial when they treated two young girls with severe combined immunodeficiency disease (inadequate immunity to bacteria and viruses). They took the girls' own white blood cells, inserted a gene they did not have that developed the needed type of immunity, and returned the cells to the subjects. Both girls improved, acquiring normal immunity, although they needed ongoing treatments.

Penn had the idea of treating a patient named Jesse Gelsinger in 1999 with a gene replacement for a defective gene preventing the ability to handle ammonia, a breakdown product of protein used by cells. Most children with this disease die in infancy, but since Jesse Gelsinger had only a partial mutation, he was able to live to the age of eighteen with diet restrictions. Penn researchers injected Jesse with an adenovirus (a virus causing the common cold) that carried the repaired gene for the gene defect. Jesse died four days later of a massive immune reaction causing multiple organ failures. What they had not told Jesse nor the FDA, was that two prior subjects had serious side effects from a similar virus used in the same way, and even more importantly, that there were many deaths in monkeys using the same system prior to the experiment with Jesse. The FDA found that Penn had lapsed in assuring the reasonable safety of gene therapy and protecting the subjects of gene therapy trials; since then Penn has taken all precautions to protect these patients. Subsequent trials have been more successful. But you need to be sure that you adhere to yours and society's values when acting on a serendipitous discovery.

A Change in the Climate

There are multiple examples of ideas or discoveries that seemed really valuable initially, then took a turn for the worse. Sometimes people lose interest. Other times the situation in the world may change, making the item less necessary. Sometimes even bad luck can doom something that had a promising future. One aspect of bad luck may be a change in the political situation in your own institution, putting your own values in conflict with the institution's, whereas at a prior time they clearly meshed. All of these changes may require you to shift gears or abandon your project altogether.

Sometimes the change in climate can affect your job. It may make it uncomfortable for you to continue at that institution or firm, or may even put you out of a job (see the next section on bad luck). Such occurrences have happened to me along the way in my career. For example, one of my positions was ideal for someone with my experience and background. The chairman of medicine was also very favorably oriented to academic general internal medicine. However, he was an interim chair, and when a permanent chairman was appointed, the climate noticeably shifted toward specialty medicine. I was told by the new chair at one point that the primary purpose of general internal medicine in academia was to refer patients to the specialists. His feeling was that academic general internists should not engage in teaching or any kind of research as that was reserved for the specialists. I therefore decided that my future was limited there and began looking elsewhere. So sometimes you need to decide if a climate change is sufficient to result in the decision to look at another job or position.

Similar situations occur in the corporate world, brought on by society's changes in attitudes. There are many products that seemed like a really good idea when brought to market, only to flop later on. Many examples exist of inventors who thought they would take advantage of a perceived need, only to find that the times and needs had changed. One of the most notable among these ideas was that of the bomb shelter. Fallout shelters for families were around since the 1950s but were never taken seriously. Only a few were purchased, usually by individuals considered to be out of the mainstream.

Then, in 1961, all of that changed. In July of that year, President Kennedy spoke on television indicating that the Soviet Union was threatening to cut off access to the purportedly free city of Berlin, and he indicated that if they did, the U.S. would respond to that in force. There were fears of the real possibility of a nuclear war when Kennedy told the audience to take shelter should it occur. Shortly thereafter, in October 1962, the U.S. and USSR really were on the brink of nuclear war when missiles with nuclear warheads were discovered in Cuba and the U.S. enacted a full blockade. The country was on edge, and individuals saw the need for a bomb shelter in their backyard or basement. Although many people constructed bomb shelters on their own, companies providing professionally made shelters sprang up, and since the shelters needed supplies to furnish them, other companies began supplying them. In all, it was estimated that the bomb shelter industry, including shelters themselves and supplies for them, could run in the (1960s era) $2 billion to $20 billion range.

So why did the bomb shelter market fizzle? For one thing, many of the shelters leaked with heavy rains, and owners would have had radioactive water irradiating them if there really was a nuclear war. The shelters were expensive, in the range of $2,000 (then almost the cost of a new automobile). More importantly, though, the realization occurred that if there truly was an all-out nuclear war, not much would be left to go to when it was all over. Clubs like "Ground Zero" sprang up, in which everyone would try to get to ground zero (the direct location of the nearest thermonuclear explosion) so it would be over quickly rather than suffering with radiation poisoning. Then as nuclear disarmament began in the 1980s and beyond, bomb shelters seemed superfluous. In all, some six hundred bomb shelter manufacturers went bankrupt. Suppliers of items for bomb shelters fared better; they turned their attention to the increasing interest in outdoor camping. But in the end, very few bomb shelters were actually ever constructed.

Sometimes some discovery seen by the public as something everyone *must* have fades over time. There are two classic examples of this from the early to mid-1960s, the time that the whole world decided to innovate (at least it seemed so to an excited kid like me). One was a "toy" for kids called "Instant Fish." An ichthyologist (fish scientist) traveling in Africa found that fish were swimming in an isolated mud puddle far from a source of fresh water. He theorized that this species of fish probably lays eggs that lie dormant in the soil until there is a storm with rainwater filling the puddle, in which case the eggs hatch. In fact, this is now known to occur in other species located in other areas. For example, while hiking in the Canyonlands National Park in eastern Utah, I was amazed to find information on the trail that indicated some areas of the slickrock (sandstone that is smooth and weathered) have potholes; when storms arrive, they fill with water and both amphibians and fairy shrimp hatch and develop.

Rather than writing a scientific article about this species of fish, the scientist contacted the Wham-O Company (yup, the same company of the Hula-Hoop fame) and contracted with them, shipping large batches of the mud containing the hibernating eggs to Wham-O, who started making Instant Fish kits. The product premiered in 1962 and was instantly a huge success. Customers bought the kits as soon as they went on the shelves. So why did it soon fizzle? Wham-O found that the fish couldn't produce eggs fast enough to stock the kits. Demand by consumers far exceeded the capability of Wham-O to produce the kits. Customers became interested in other toys that appeared on the market, and the Instant Fish kits lost interest. It was another fad that lasted only a short time in the sixties.

One other crazy fad in the 1960s that was initially a hit and then fizzled was paper dresses. Scott Paper Company had developed a color line of paper towels, paper napkins and toilet paper, and wanted to promote the line to the public. The company came up with the idea of paper dresses, which were sleeveless shifts, available in only paisley and op art prints. They were treated for fire resistance and had a textured surface. Scott offered the dresses as a mail order for $1.25; each dress could be worn three to ten times. In the first six months Scott received 500,000 orders. The fashion industry went wild, yet Scott discontinued production after meeting the 500,000 orders as the company wasn't interested in dress manufacturing (more about that later). Mars Manufacturing Corporation in Asheville, North Carolina, sold 80,000 dresses per week. Other companies introduced unique variations on a theme: Sterling Paper Products introduced maternity and wedding dresses, a $12 man's suit, and even resort wear, including a (gasp!) paper bikini which was "specially treated." Various stores like Joseph Magnin Company and Abraham & Strauss opened special boutiques to carry the paper dress lines.

Paper dresses seemed to be the very big wave of the future, yet the fad lasted only a few short years. Paper tended to balloon out in places where it shouldn't be ballooning, and they had limited wearability. The public lost interest in the fad, as so often occurs. The only paper clothing you can still find is in hospitals (gowns and the like).

A Change in Luck

Sometimes luck (in these cases, bad luck) has to do with whether a job, idea, or invention goes nowhere from the start or dies a quiet death after seeming to be something of value. Bad luck can sometimes be a change in an institution that convinces you to leave your current job for another, or may even doom your employment there. I have had the good fortune of being employed as a faculty member in internal medicine, so my career, luckily, has never been "doomed"; yet changes in former workplaces have motivated me to leave my job on multiple occasions. Two examples readily come to mind.

The first occurred in the mid-1980s. I was the internal residency program director at a hospital in Philadelphia, enjoying leading a very successful program. I was able to administrate the program and do a lot of the teaching and interacting with the residents. They had a great deal of respect for me, as did the chairman of medicine there. I was lucky to have found this position; I was discussing aspects of resident education with a friend at a general internal medicine meeting when he happened to mention that it was a shame that their internal medicine residency program director had just left. I got the idea that, since I was so interested in teaching, running a residency program might be the ideal job for me. I applied for the position, interviewed, and was selected.

The way recruitment for a residency program works is that in the autumn a large number of applicants send in their applications, which are reviewed, and then the best are selected to come for interviews. Then, in the early winter, all of the residency programs list in order the fourth-year medical students whom they would like to join the residency program the following July, and the students all list in order the programs they would most like to join. All of this information goes into a large national data bank, with a computer then matching the students with the programs to which they have been assigned. In mid-March, the programs find out whether they have filled all of the slots in the residency program they are offering (we call it matching) or whether they have unfilled slots. Better programs matched, while less desirable programs went unfilled. These events always occurred on a Friday.

Prior to the mid-eighties, internal medicine was a highly sought after residency program compared to some others, so that even lesser programs usually filled all of their slots. Then, in the mid-eighties, the values of students seeking residency programs changed. Medical students in the 60s and 70s were concerned mostly with how they could serve the public. This was a legacy from the Kennedy era. But by the 80s, with student debt sky-rocketing and a desire to have a better lifestyle, students became more interested in better paying and less time consuming specialties than general internal medicine. The year was 1986, and that year match day was known as "Black Friday." Students' interest in internal medicine plummeted; many programs went unfulfilled and had to seek out less qualified applicants who would be available after the match. This happened at the hospital at which I was the residency director just like it did at multiple other institutions, but the chairman of medicine was reluctant to believe that such a wholesale change had occurred, and instead believed that I had somehow turned off the applicants. He therefore sought out and appointed a "director of medical education" to oversee all of the operations of the residency program, i.e., take away all of the autonomy and responsibility I had for the administration of the program. The director of medical education began making rules that I could not live with and therefore I could not enforce, causing me to look for another job. Even though I'd found the job in a serendipitous way, an unlikely incident forced me to change direction.

The second change occurred while I was at a Veterans Affairs Medical Center. I had been there since 1991 as the co-chief of general internal medicine and was faculty at one of the nearby universities. I had the luxury of assisting in the running of our division, representing the general internal medicine faculty both at the parent organization, as well as at the VA, and had a great deal of teaching and research responsibilities along with some patient care. It was again an ideal job for me. Unfortunately, there were a number of political and economic changes happening in the late 1990s in medicine and specifically amongst some of the area medical schools. The university at which I was faculty was one of those having some financial difficulties, so the decision was made to divest itself of any costs and residency slots they could not afford. The logical choice was to pull out of the VA, since another institution ran most of those programs anyway.

We met with the chairman of medicine at my parent university, who assured me that the faculty I represented at the VA would still have positions. When the university was about to pull out of the VA, I was shuffled back and forth from the chairman of medicine to the division chief of general internal medicine, with no one offering up funds to secure our positions. I was livid, as I had been lied to by the chairman and unsupported by our division chief. I knew I couldn't force the issue. Without any recourse, and unwilling to have a position that did not have any teaching or research responsibilities attached, I immediately began searching. At a general internal medicine meeting, I happened upon a position at Christiana Care Health System in Wilmington, Delaware, which I ended up enjoying for ten years. So bad luck can end up being an unexpected event and serendipitous, as this one was. But it can also affect one's job, and you have to be ready to decide what to do should that occur.

Bad luck can certainly also affect the corporate world. Some of the other ideas in this chapter, such as the Instant Fish kit, had an element of this in their decline from fame. However, two examples are directly related to just bad luck. The first was the Dymaxion car developed by R. Buckminster Fuller. The first prototype was created on July 12, 1933, way ahead of its time. It was a streamlined, oval car with plenty of large, wide windows so the driver could have maximum vision of the road and the surroundings (there was even a periscope that projected through the roof). The car had three wheels: two in front for traction and one in the rear for steering, similar to the rudder on a ship. The car could make a 360-degree turn in its own length and could therefore park in extremely tight spaces, yet could seat eleven people. Fuller extensively tested the car and found that it was unstable at high speeds due to the rear wheel steering and its aerodynamic shape. It was brought out at the 1933 Chicago World's Fair, at which it would speed across the floor of the transportation exhibition hall, then suddenly stop and make a 360-degree turn. He was planning on further work before the car could be released to the public. People were awed, and one would think that there would have been a tremendous interest in it.

Nope. Bad luck struck the car (literally). Just outside the grounds of the World's Fair, another car accidentally hit the rear end of the Dymaxion car, which went out of control and rolled over. This was likely not due to the rear wheel steering, since it became unstable only at high speeds, which was not the case in this crash. However, the driver was killed (no seat belts at that time) and the passengers in the car were seriously injured. The other vehicle was driven away before the press arrived, and therefore the assumption was that the Dymaxion car was unstable even at slow speeds, causing it to roll over. Headlines the next day announced that the car had caused the death of the driver. So, no interest was ever generated in the Dymaxion car, despite Fuller's attempts to disprove the assumption that the car was unstable.

Another innovation that didn't go anywhere was homes made out of polyurethane foam in the 1970s. Bob Masters and Roy Mason promoted the foam homes, touting them as the home of the future. The foam was sprayed onto chicken wire structures in most cases, though Masters and Mason also sprayed it onto giant, vinyl, balloon-like structures to create rounded rooms fashioned into a house. They went around the country building these showcase homes with the expectation that they would really catch on, leading to their fame and fortune.

So what happened? There are no foam homes today, you will notice. Yet these homes would allow one to have all kinds of free expression as to the dimension, and more importantly the shape, of the individual rooms along with the house as a whole. Well, one creates polyurethane foam by mixing urethane liquid with formaldehyde, and when sprayed it expands by thirty times its volume and hardens. This particular combination involving formaldehyde, which was used in insulation of traditional houses along with the foam homes, led to some health concerns in the 1980s. Polyurethane is toxic as a liquid, but becomes inert as a solid. Similarly, formaldehyde, though a respiratory toxin, dissipates when mixed with urethane to create polyurethane. Polyurethane is flammable but can be treated with fire retardants. This information was publicized, and people became afraid of the nontoxic solidified form as well as the toxic liquid. The homes therefore did not catch on with the public. In addition, it is probably a good thing that they were not built in large numbers, as by the 1990s most had to be torn down since they were crumbling so badly.

Sometimes a really great innovation or invention doesn't take off because something comes along that is better and/or cheaper. Remember *2001: A Space Odyssey* from 1968? In the film one of the astronauts receives a broadcast birthday greeting from his parents on Earth while he is out beyond Mars. The idea came from the actual development of the Picturephone by AT&T, which was unveiled in New York City at the 1964 World's Fair. AT&T promised that soon there would be locations in New York City, Chicago, and Washington, D.C. where one could use a Picturephone to call and *see* someone else in one of the other three locations. The problem was that the Picturephone required 125 circuits compared to one circuit for a regular call due to the density of information being transmitted. Thus, even though such a device would have certain value (for example, when a salesman was demonstrating a product for a company), a call from New York to Chicago in 1964 would cost $21 for three minutes, compared with $1.35 for a regular phone call. Additionally, the device was inconvenient, given that it was in only three locations. AT&T again experimented with the Picturephone in 1970 without success, and then in the 1980s Sony and Mitsubishi experimented with it. Although some corporations invested in videoconferencing technology in the early 1990s, it was expensive (the equipment cost up to $25,000) and limited in scope. AT&T invented the VideoPhone 2500 in 1992, a flip-up phone that had a color video screen. It used signal compression to limit the number of circuits required. However, the quality of the image was limited (it transmitted at ten frames per second) and one unit cost $1,500. Thus, interest even in this technology was limited.

We obviously did not give up, despite the bad luck that pestered AT&T and others. Despite the claim by Paul Kirchner in his 1995 book *Forgotten Fads and Fabulous Flops* that communication did not need visual transmission, it is hard to imagine our world without Skype or Google Chat on our computers, or our ubiquitous smartphones with video capability. The revolution in computers and communication technology far outdistanced the beginning attempts at videoconferencing of the 1960s through the 1980s. Sometimes technology will make obsolete an earlier, promising innovation or invention.

A Change in You

Sometimes your values, attitudes, or interests might change, causing you to have to make a decision about whether to continue with an innovation, invention, or job, or to reach out for something else. Most often what occurs is that some opportunities arise in an area in which you may or may not have expertise, and you have a decision to make. Examples abound in the fortunes of corporations and individuals, and here are a few which I have recently come across, including my own.

I have changed directions in my career several times. The first time was the direction my research took early on. I was initially most interested in not only teaching about patient-physician communication but also doing research in the field. My first experiences at UConn led me to be interested in particular about how patient-physician communication impacted patient medication adherence. However, when I became interested in medical ethics due to my serendipitous exposure at Hahnemann University (see Chapter 2), the research aspects of my career shifted. Most of my subsequent work quantitatively explored the attitudes and values of patients and physicians encountering ethical dilemmas, rather than that of mainstream communication topics. I did explore some aspects of communication later on, such as the issues of boundaries in the patient-physician relationship, and some that involved both communication and ethics. But most of it related strictly to medical ethics.

Another change involved the bookends of my time at the University of California, San Diego. My decision to join the faculty occurred in 2006 and became reality in 2007. My wife and I had resided on the East Coast all of our lives, and I was really happy at Christiana Care Health System in Wilmington, Delaware. But two of our children lived out in California, and I really was longing to do some in-classroom medical school teaching (all of my teaching involved precepting in the clinical setting, i.e., teaching students and internal medicine residents as they interacted with patients either in the office or in the hospital). The opportunity that I serendipitously came across was what set the wheels in motion. But before that, I had made a change; I decided

I'd had enough of East Coast winters and wanted more small-group, on-campus university teaching. So I jumped at the chance to have a warmer climate and a greater teaching opportunity.

The other side of my UCSD experience came about more recently when I serendipitously came across the opportunities to be a docent at the San Diego Air & Space Museum, a consultant for the communication skills company called the SullivanLuallin Group, and the author of this book. With all of those things enticing me, and the growing emphasis in medical institutions on computer and administrative work, which consumes some of the time available for interaction with the patient, I decided that the time was right to make the move to retirement.

As an individual, the most famous astronaut, Neil Armstrong, had a choice to make in March 1962, only a short time after his two-year-old daughter's death from a brain tumor. At that time, he was employed by NASA and was working at the Edwards High-Speed Flight Station in California. He was flying the X-15, a rocket-propelled plane that tested hypersonic (above Mach 5) flight at the fringes of space, and could have continued to stay with that project. However, he was also working on the Dyna-Soar project for the Air Force. Armstrong was one of only six pilots who were slotted to fly the Dyna-Soar when it launched. Dyna-Soar was a winged space plane that the Air Force wanted to use for testing and use in orbit. Finally, Armstrong had heard about NASA's call for an astronaut class that would be involved in the Apollo program.

Armstrong had an important decision to make regarding his career. He later stated that there was a growing national interest in manned space flight since John Glenn had orbited the Earth the previous month. Glenn was given a ticker tape parade down Broadway in New York City, and the whole nation was going wild over the prospect of heading toward the moon. Armstrong wanted to be part of that, and decided to trade his love of test-pilot, high-speed flights for the chance to fly into space. He therefore submitted his application to NASA. As they say, the rest is history. He was in the right places and the right circumstances to be the first man to set foot on the moon. But what if he had made one of the other two choices? The X-15 flights did continue for a while, but they were phased out by 1968. And the Dyna-Soar project (I actually did build a model of the vehicle when I was a kid) never got off the ground. Neil Armstrong obviously made the right decision. This wasn't about making a choice based on which program would be successful, but rather a change in Neil Armstrong's interests.

In the corporate arena, Lockheed Aerospace Corporation (before it merged with Martin to become Lockheed Martin) in the 1920s and '30s was very successful in manufacturing airplanes of a medium size but with long range. It was famous for the Lockheed Vega (the airplane that Amelia Earhart used to become the first woman to fly solo across the Atlantic), the Electra Model 10 (the two-engine, larger transport airplane in which she was lost on her around-the-world attempt), and the Model 12 Electra Junior and Model 14 Super Electra. They had never delved into the military side of aircraft before. But during World War II, there was no demand for commercial planes. Rather, the United States was looking for aircraft manufacturers to produce military aircraft. Lockheed would have fared badly financially if it continued with only its commercial planes. So when the U.S. put out a call for an interceptor (fighter plane), Lockheed utilized the skills of Kelly Johnson, one of the world's leading aircraft design engineers, to submit the prototype for the P-38 Lightning. This plane eventually became one of the most prolific and successful fighters of the war.

Lockheed also manufactured B-17 Flying Fortress bombers along with British Venturas and Hudson bombers. It ranked tenth in wartime aircraft production. The die was cast: After the war Kelly Johnson and his Skunk Works (a secret design group who developed many advanced military aircraft, named after a cartoon character in *Li'l Abner*) produced such planes as the U-2 spy plane and then A-12 and SR-71 reconnaissance planes, which were tremendously successful. Lockheed did produce the Constellation ("Connie") and Super Constellation ("Super Connie") in the 1950s, and later the L-1011 wide-body passenger jet, but the majority of its aircraft production (it later got into satellites, including the Hubble Telescope) was for the military. Thus, Lockheed availed itself of the opportunity to reap the benefits of military contracts, a choice it made back in 1940. Its alternative was to continue with commercial airplanes only, but it probably would have been a poor decision financially. So these corporate and personal decisions were voluntary. That often occurs; not all of the "know when to fold 'em" situations are forced upon us. Often they are opportunities that we may want to take advantage of instead.

CHAPTER 11
WHAT DO I DO WITH IT?

Once you have your idea or discovery in hand and have brought it to the point of being promoted and possibly sold to the public, you need to decide where you are going to go from there. Much of it depends on the situation you find yourself in. First, is the product or idea profitable (monetarily or otherwise)? The second factor is whether you have the interest, skills, and resources (money, time, space, equipment, et cetera) to continue its manufacture or promotion. I can't give you specific recommendations, but here are some guidelines that may be of use to you in your decision-making. In this chapter, I will reexamine many of the examples we previously saw, looking at how and when to sell rights to a discovery or invention and how one must have persistence and sometimes a second idea to make an idea or invention profitable.

For Sale

Assuming that you have a product as a result of your serendipitous event (rather than an idea, career, or personal opportunity), and that the product is popular and profitable, the decision often comes down to whether to sell the patent and rights to a larger firm or to continue the manufacturing yourself. This is really a personal decision, and there are examples of both decisions in the annals of discoveries. It depends on how invested you are in the product and whether you wish to continue to spend the majority of your time with it, or whether it makes sense to sell and use the income for other purposes (another product, philanthropy, retirement, et cetera). But generally if it *is* profitable, there should be no real difficulty in selling it to someone else.

Selling it later in the development is always possible. We previously explored the story of Ben & Jerry's ice cream, and how the founders hit upon a very popular and profitable idea. Later on, while they were in their late forties, they were offered $326 million twenty-two years after they started the company with only one ice cream parlor. They remain active in the company, but in a consulting role with no authority or responsibility. Both have used their time and money in later years in social activism. So it is possible to continue with the product from your serendipitous discovery for quite a while if you have the interest, ability, and resources, selling only when it makes sense to do so from a personal point of view.

Others pulled the plug earlier for monetary gain from the patent, or for a contract with a larger manufacturing company. The way a patent works is that once you have invented or discovered something, you apply for a patent in the U.S. Patent Office (it is important to have a patent attorney for this process). The patent office does a search to be sure nothing like your creation has ever been patented before. Once assured that yours is unique, it is given a patent that protects it from someone else copying your idea without giving you royalties, that is, part of the money from sales. You can also sell the right to have someone else manufacture your product, with you getting a negotiated part of the net sales. Remember the cellophane guy (Chapter 3) and the Toll House Cookie gal (Chapter 2)? Well, Jacques Brandenberger, the creator of cellophane, encountered his unexpected event at the restaurant in 1908, but he worked with it until 1920 when he was finally able to obtain the patent for cellophane. At that point he started producing products such as eye shields and gas masks. But after only three years, he licensed the patent for cellophane to DuPont so that it could be made and sold in the United States and Central America. Within four years DuPont found a way to make cellophane not only waterproof but also moisture-proof by adding a layer of nitrocellulose. Sales of the product tripled at that point. So Brandenberger basically got out of the business early in its development.

Similarly, Ruth Graves Wakefield got a deal from the manufacture of Toll House cookies early in her career. After serendipitously discovering the product in 1930 and selling it only at their inn known as the Toll House, she negotiated a forty-year contract with Nestle after a salesman happened to stop by and try the cookie. The contract allowed Wakefield to use the Toll House name for the cookie, and she was given a lifetime supply of Nestle morsels (chocolate chips), while Nestle was allowed to print the recipe for Toll House cookies on its bags of chocolate morsels. Wakefield continued to operate the Toll House Inn, serving Toll

House cookies in addition to her lobster dinners and other dishes, and she wrote a best-selling cookbook with her recipes from the Toll House Inn that went through thirty-nine printings. So when you discover or invent something, be sure to get a patent. You can then decide, if and when you want, to sell the rights to the patent or negotiate a contract with a large manufacturer.

But What If It's a Bust?

No one wishes for your idea, invention, or discovery to go bust, and I certainly don't want to dwell upon it, but sometimes it happens. Here are some useful tips if it should happen. One of the more important is to learn and get ideas from the process. Even if the invention doesn't seem like it will be a success, there are ways in which it can be made productive.

For example, we explored the bust that was foam houses in the previous chapter. They never amounted to much due to the scare regarding health risks from formaldehyde and polyurethane, their weird shapes, and the lack of permanence. But maybe they could be found to have some use. There has been a great increase in concern over housing for the homeless in San Diego, as well as in other cities. Foam houses can now be made with polyurethane that does not contain formaldehyde. Might this be a means of supplying housing for those without homes? I don't know if anyone has considered this, but city administrators are welcome to consider my idea. Other ideas or inventions which did not pan out might occasionally find uses. And, when you look at most of the inventions or ideas in this book that "went bust," most of them still reaped a good deal of fame and profit for their inventor before they went under.

BIBLIOGRAPHY

100 Scientific Discoveries That Changed the World. Washington, D.C.: National Geographic, 2012.

Bertolero, Max and D. S. Bassett. "How Matter Becomes Mind." *Scientific American.* 2019, vol. 321: 26-33.

Betsworth, Deborah G. and J. C. Hansen. "The Categorization of Serendipitous Career Development Events." *Journal of Career Assessment.* 1996, vol. 4: 91-98.

Chetwynd, Josh. *How the Hot Dog Found Its Bun.* Guilfors, Connecticut: Lyons Press, 2012.

Decharne, Max. *Vulgar Tongues.* New York: Pegasus Books Ltd, 2017.

Dobelli, Rolf. *The Art of Thinking Clearly.* New York: Harper Collins Publishers, 2013.

Donner-Banzhoff, Norbert. "Solving the Diagnostic Challenge: A Patient-Centered Approach." *Annals of Family Medicine.* 2018, vol. 16: 353-358.

Elborough, Travis. *Atlas of the Unexpected*. London, UK: White Lion Publishing, 2018.

Farber, Neil J., B.M. Aboff, J. Weiner, et al. "Physicians' Willingness to Participate in the Process of Lethal Injection for Capital Punishment." *Annals of Internal Medicine*. 2001, vol. 135: 884-888.

Farber, Neil J., M.S. Berger, E.B. Davis, et al. "Confidentiality and Health Insurance Fraud." *Archives of Internal Medicine*. 1997, vol. 157: 501-504.

Farber, Neil J., J. Castellano, J. Weiner, and E.G. Boyer. "Physicians' Understanding of Consent Requirements for Phase I Clinical Trials in Cognitively Impaired or Highly Vulnerable Patients." *Accountability in Research*. 2004, vol. 11: 63-78.

Farber, Neil J., E.B. Davis, J. Weiner, et al. "Physicians' Attitudes About Involvement in Lethal Injection for Capital Punishment." *Archives of Internal Medicine*. 2000, vol. 160: 2912-2916.

Farber, Neil J., H.T. Farber, J. Weiner, et al. "Telling Patients About the Diagnosis of HIV Infection." *Journal of General Internal Medicine*. 1996, vol. 11: 494-496.

Farber, Neil J., A. Friedland, B.M. Aboff, et al. "Using Patients with Cancer to Educate Residents About Giving Bad News." *Journal of Palliative Care*. 2003, vol. 19: 54-57.

Farber, Neil J., S.G. Gilbert, B.M. Aboff, et al. "Physicians' Willingness to Report Impaired Colleagues." *Social Science & Medicine*. 2005, vol. 61:L 1772-1775.

ABOUT THE AUTHOR

 Neil J. Farber is a Professor Emeritus of Clinical Medicine at University of California, San Diego, and a docent at the San Diego Air & Space Museum. He has been an academic internal medicine physician for 40 years, teaching, researching and providing patient care in medical schools initially on the East Coast. For the past 12 years, he was Professor of Clinical Medicine at University of California, San Diego, retiring at the end of April 2019. He has received numerous awards, including Top Doctor of San Diego five times, and is a member of the FDA Non-Prescription Drug Advisory Committee. He has published over 60 research papers and has had a multitude of serendipitous events occur,which have significantly (and positively) influenced his career and his personal life.

Printed in Great Britain
by Amazon

59696360R00135